PORTFOLIO OF BASKETBALL DRILLS FROM COLLEGE COACHES

PORTFOLIO OF BASKETBALL DRILLS FROM COLLEGE COACHES

Roger Haun, Editor

Parker Publishing Co., Inc. • West Nyack, N.Y.

Library of Congress Cataloging in Publication Data
Main entry under title:

Portfolio of basketball drills from college coaches.

1. Basketball—Training. I. Haun, Roger.
GV885.35.P67 1985 796.32′363′077 85-3463

ISBN 0-13-685785-X

Printed in the United States of America

To my girls: my Wife, Nancy, and my Daughters, Rachel and Rebekah, who have put up with my long hours away from home as I worked on this book and pursued my coaching career

Acknowledgments

A special thanks to the great coaches who took time from their busy schedules to contribute a drill to make this book a reality. It has been a privilege for me to be associated with them in this project.

And to my mother who took the time to type parts of this manuscript

Editor's Note: The number of years in coaching and the coaches' won/loss records that appear in the coaches' summaries are accurate through the 1983–84 season.

INTRODUCTION

Portfolio of Basketball Drills from College Coaches is written in a manner to help you and your players perfect the fundamentals of the game. Its purpose is to enable you to build a successful program or to continue your winning tradition, as it has for the coaches who have contributed to this book.

One hundred twenty college coaches from all over the nation, including some of the best—James Valvano from North Carolina State University, Ralph Miller from Oregon State University and Lute Olson from the University of Arizona—have contributed their favorite drills and techniques for improving the various aspects of the game of basketball.

Ball handling, conditioning, defense, individual development, the fast break, rebounding, shooting, and team development all have complete sections. These sections include a diagram of each drill, an explanation of how to execute each drill, and the coach who contributed the drill.

Although not guaranteed to produce 20 wins a season, *Portfolio of Basketball Drills from College Coaches* will definitely add quality and variation to the grind of daily practice schedules.

CONTENTS

PART I BALL HANDLING DRILLS

PART II CONDITIONING DRILLS

PART III DEFENSIVE DRILLS

KEY

O - Offensive Player
X - Defensive Player
C - Coach
M - Manager
R - Rebounder
P - Passer
● - Ball
□ - Cone or Pylon
——→ - Player Movement
——| - Pick or Box Out
——(- Defensive Pick-up or Take a Charge
- - - -→ - Chest Pass
- - = - -→ - Bounce Pass
- - = - -→ - Overhead Pass
∿∿∿→ - Dribbling
·······→ - Shot
ooooo→ - Ball Rolling
∼∼→ - Defensive Slide

Part I

BALL HANDLING DRILLS

COACH JOE MILLER—METHODIST COLLEGE

Coach Miller has been coaching for twenty-three years. Nineteen of those twenty-three have been at the college level either as an assistant or a head coach. As an assistant coach at Ohio Northern University, he compiled a won/lost record of 104 wins and 58 losses. His 1976–77 Methodist College team won the Dixie Intercollegiate Athletic Conference championship and tournament and finished with an 18–8 record. They repeated the OIAC championship win the following year as well. He was named OIAC Coach of the Year in 1977.

PIVOT AND DRIVE DRILL

Purpose: To develop pivoting and penetrating techniques
Personnel and Equipment Needed: A coach or manager, a minimum of three players, one basketball and a basket
Teaching Points: 1) Pivot under control, stay low and wide. 2) Have players drive in various directions. 3) Concentrate on the lay-up.

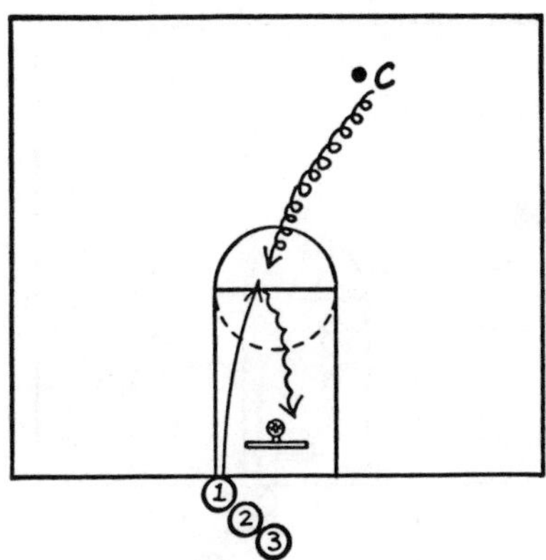

Directions: Have the players form one line underneath the basket. The coach or manager is out at the center circle with the ball and begins the drill by rolling the ball to the free throw line. The first player in line sprints to the free throw line and picks up the ball. He then pivots and faces the basket (he can do either a reverse or forward pivot). The coach then gives him the direction he wants him to drive. The player can go straight to the basket or cross over depending on his pivot foot. He should make a good power move to the basket.

COACH EDDIE BURKE—DREXEL UNIVERSITY

Coach Burke has been in college coaching for six years. He has achieved a won/lost record of 90 wins and 76 losses at Drexel University.

GO TO THE WELL DRILL

Purpose: To improve the skills necessary to drive hard to the basket
Personnel and Equipment Needed: A minimum of three players, two basketballs and a basket
Teaching Points: 1) Dribble hard—keep the ball low. 2) Use a reverse pivot. 3) Make your drive straight do not circle or loop. 4) Concentrate on the basket, not the dribbling.

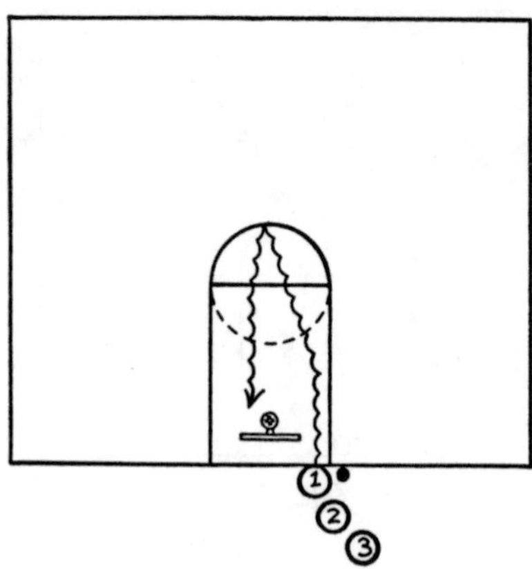

Directions: Have the players line up under the basket behind the end line. O1 dribbles the ball out to the top of the key. At this point he plants his pivot foot and makes a reverse pivot and heads to the basket for a lay-up. O2 starts when O1 has passed the bottom of the jump circle on his way to the basket. O3 takes the ball out of the net after O1's shot and goes when O2 passes the bottom of the jump circle. O1 goes to the end of the line after his lay-up. This drill should be done three times each way (right-hand reverse pivot and lay-up and left-hand reverse pivot and lay-up).

COACH KEN MARTIN—COKER COLLEGE

Coach Martin has been coaching for eleven years. Two of those eleven have been at the college level. He has an overall won/lost record of 149 wins and 120 losses. His teams made high school state play-offs in Georgia five straight years. He coached the Georgia All-Stars in 1978 and was named Coach of the Year in his region five times.

DRIBBLING STATIONS DRILL

Purpose: To improve weak hand performance and confidence
Personnel and Equipment Needed: An entire team of players, two basketballs for each player and the entire floor
Teaching Points: 1) Head-up. 2) Always keep the ball below the elbow on the dribble. 3) Pivot on the whirl or reverse dribble. 4) Use finger tips, not palms.
Directions: Have the team divide up evenly into each of the four lines shown in the diagram.

1) The first player in line number one will dribble two balls forward down the court pushing both balls out at the same time. He will come back forward but will alternate pushing the balls out. Upon completion, he will go to the end of line number two.

2) The first player in line number two will dribble both balls as he makes a defensive slide down the court and back. He should face the same sideline both down and back. Keep the lead ball out in front and do not cross over the legs. Upon completion he advances to the end of line three.

3) The first player in line three will dribble both balls down the court and back backwards. Keep the balls wide of the feet and take short steps. When he is finished he will go to the end of line four.

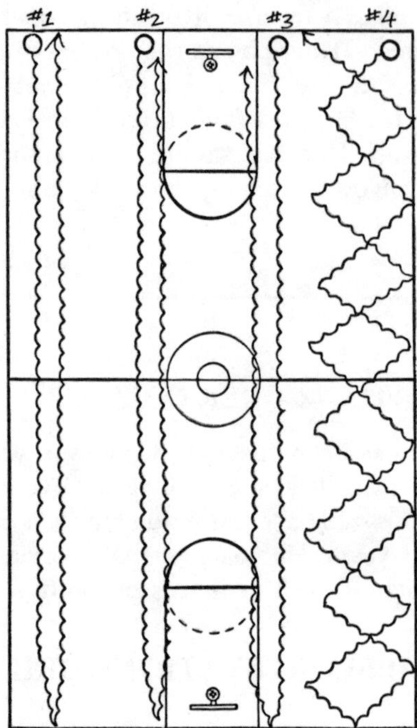

4) The first player in line four will dribble both balls down the floor and back using the whirl or reverse dribble. When he finishes, he advances to the end of line one.

All the players should be active throughout the entire drill so that those waiting in each of the lines should be doing ball handling drills while they wait. Each player should go down and back two times in each line before the drill is completed.

COACH TOM VILLEMURE—GRAND VALLEY STATE

Coach Villemure has been coaching for twenty-two years. Fourteen of those twenty-two have been at the college level. He has a won/lost record of 204 wins and 105 losses at Grand Valley and 342 wins and 150 losses overall. His team won the NAIA District III championship in 1977 and made it to the final four at the NAIA national tournament that same year. His 1976–77 team has the distinction of being the first and only four-year college team in the State of Michigan to win thirty games in a season. He has received Coach of the Year awards on four different occasions.

OUTLET—LAY-UP DRILL

Purpose: To teach the proper outlet pass and how to make a lay-up off the pass
Personnel and Equipment Needed: Minimum of five players, one basketball and a basket
Teaching Points: 1) On rebound, pivot to the outside and make a good outlet pass. 2) Be ready to receive the pass on the move. 3) Catch the ball with the finger tips, not the palms of the hand.

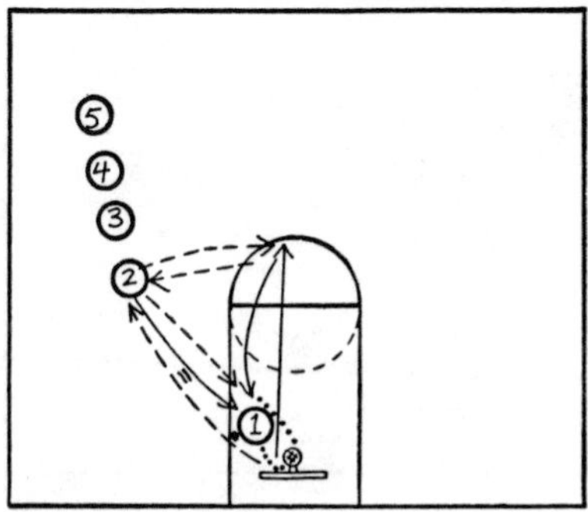

Directions: Have the players line up behind each other on the wing. O1 starts the drill by tossing the ball up on the board and rebounding that toss. He then turns to the outside and outlets the ball to O2. After he outlets the ball, he sprints to the top of the key and receives a return pass from O2. He then passes the ball back to O2 and sprints to the basket. O2 passes the ball back to O1 and follows his pass to rebound the made or missed shot by O1. O2 continues the drill and O1 goes to the end of the line. Each player should go three times on each side.

COACH BOB HUGGINS—WALSH COLLEGE

Coach Huggins has been coaching for six years at the college level. He has a won/lost record of 71 wins and 26 losses. His team was Mid-

Ohio Conference champion. He was named Coach of the Year in the Mid-Ohio Conference and in NAIA District 22.

BULL IN THE RING DRILL

Purpose: To learn to use proper passing lanes
Personnel and Equipment Needed: A minimum of three players and a basketball
Teaching Points: 1) If the defender's hand is down, take it lower with a fake and throw the pass right off the ear. 2) If the defender's hand is high, take it higher with a fake and then throw a bounce pass.

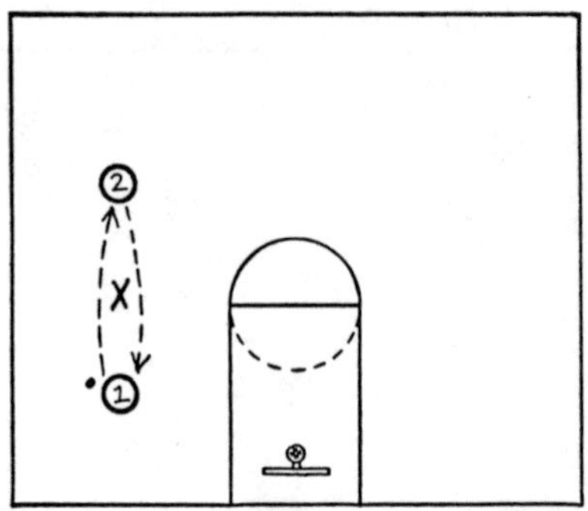

Directions: Have a defensive player between two offensive players. The defender is to attack the ball. The offensive player must pass the ball to the other offensive player without the defender touching it. If the pass is successfully made to the other offensive player, the defender will attack him. If the defender does touch the ball, the offensive player who made the bad pass switches places with the defender. The drill can continue for as long as designated.

COACH HAROLD MURRELL—ATHENS STATE COLLEGE

Coach Murrell has been coaching for eighteen years. Ten of those eighteen have been at the college level. He has an overall won/lost record of 321 wins and 185 losses. His teams won the Southern States Conference championship two years. He was named Southern States Conference Coach of the Year in 1981 and 1982. He was also named Small College Coach of the Year in Alabama in 1982.

CIRCLE PASSING DRILL

Purpose: To improve passing and catching skills and timing
Personnel and Equipment Needed: A minimum of six players, one basketball
Teaching Points: 1) Make a good pass with the proper fundamentals (step toward your receiver, snap the wrists and concentrate on the target). 2) For the tipping—finger tip control, and use both hands.

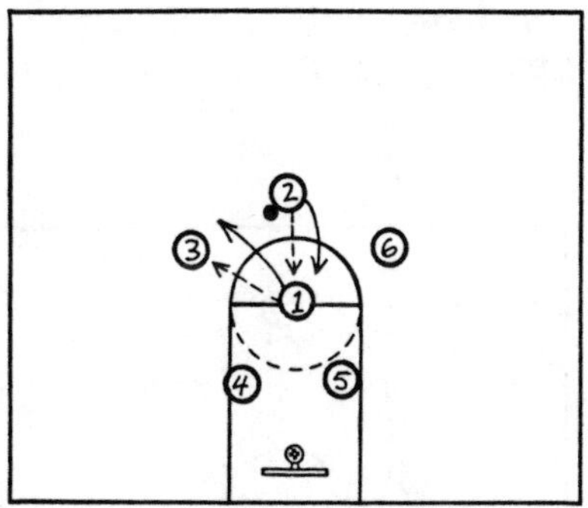

Directions: Have the players form a circle with one player inside the circle as shown. The ball starts on the outside of the circle with O2. O2 passes the ball to O1 and follows his pass inside going to his left. O1 passes the ball out to O3 and follows his pass out going to his left. O3 then passes the ball into the circle to O2 who has replaced O1. This procedure continues around the circle until everyone has been inside the circle. You can use all three types of passes (chest, bounce and overhead). You can end the drill by having the players tip the ball instead of passing it. You should use both hands on the tip.

Variation: Make a larger circle and have two players on the inside with their backs to each other and two balls on the outside of the circle opposite them. The drill runs the same, only now you have two balls going.

COACH BILLY LEE—PEMBROKE STATE UNIVERSITY

Coach Lee has been coaching for eleven years. Five of those eleven have been at the college level. He has achieved a won/lost record of 74 wins and 72 losses at Pembroke State. His teams won back-to-back Carolinas Conference championships in 1981 and 1982.

PRESSURE PASSING DRILL

Purpose: To teach passing under pressure and passing through the defense
Personnel and Equipment Needed: One coach, a minimum of four players, one basketball and a basket
Teaching Points: 1) Make sure passer pivots hard, slashing the ball. 2) Make a good crisp pass. 3) Take a good power lay-up.

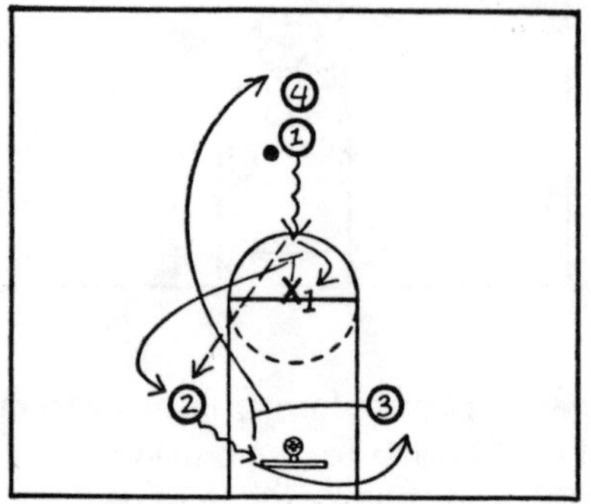

Directions: Position one player on each side of the key at the blocks (O2 and O3). Have a defensive player at the free throw line (X1). Then have the rest of the team line up at the top of the key (O1). O1 starts the drill by dribbling up to meet X1. X1 forces him to pick up his dribble and puts extreme pressure on him. O1 pivots and slashes the ball to protect it. This is done until the coach points to a receiver (O2 and O3), O2 in this case. O1 passes to O2 and O3 comes over to defend against O2 who makes a power lay-up. The rotation of players is as follows: O3 goes to the end of the line, O2 becomes O3, X1 becomes O2, O1 becomes X1 and O4 is the new O1.

Variation: Have two defenders at the free throw line to meet the dribbler. In this drill allow the passer to decide whom to pass to.

COACH ORIN SCHUELER—SIOUX FALLS COLLEGE

Coach Schueler has been coaching for twenty-three years. Three of those twenty-three have been at the college level. He has an overall won/lost record of 297 wins and 177 losses. His teams have won several tournament and conference championships and his 1976 team won the South Dakota High School Class A state championship.

FOUR PLAYER PASSING DRILL

Purpose: To improve passing skills, quickness and timing
Personnel and Equipment Needed: A minimum of eight players, one basketball and a basket
Teaching Points: 1) Make sharp passes. 2) Use the proper pivot on the outlet pass. 3) Make a hard cut to the basket.

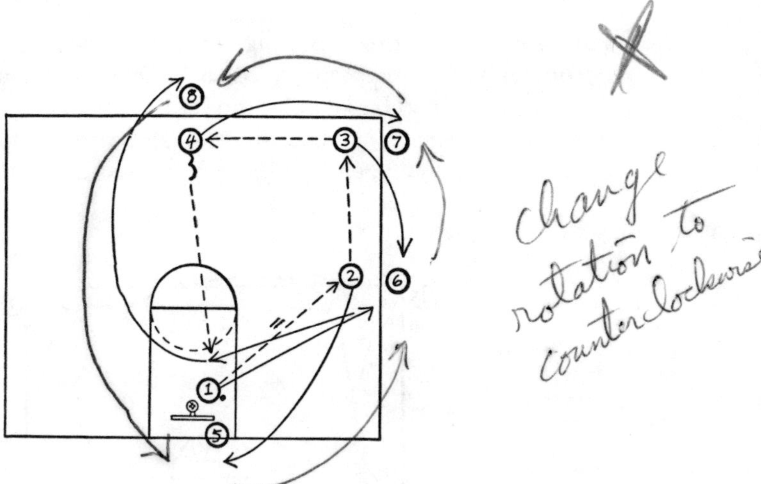

Directions: Divide the players into four groups and position them as diagrammed. O1 begins the drill by tossing the ball up off the board and rebounding it. He then outlets the ball to O2. O2 passes the ball to O3. O3 then passes to O4. O4 takes two dribbles and will pass the ball to O1.

While the ball is being passed, O1 sprints and touches the sideline at the free throw line extended and returns quickly for the pass from O4. O1 shoots a lay-up and the next player in line (O5) rebounds the ball and continues the drill. The players rotate to the different lines in a counter-clockwise fashion (O1 goes to the end of O4's line, O4 to the end of O3's line, O3 to the end of O2's line and O2 to the end of O1's line. Continue the drill for a determined amount of time.

COACH STAN SIMPSON—MIDDLE TENNESSEE STATE UNIVERSITY

Coach Simpson has been coaching for twenty-three years. Thirteen of those twenty-three have been at the college level. He has an overall won/lost record of 419 wins and 125 losses. His teams won two state high school championships and one Ohio Valley Conference championship. He was named Georgia High School Coach of the Year in 1971.

FOUR CORNER PASSING DRILL

Purpose: To improve passing techniques, timing and conditioning
Personnel and Equipment Needed: One coach, an entire team of players, one or two basketballs and half the floor
Teaching Points: 1) Make sharp crisp passes. 2) Come to meet the pass. 3) Occasionally, change the type of pass used.

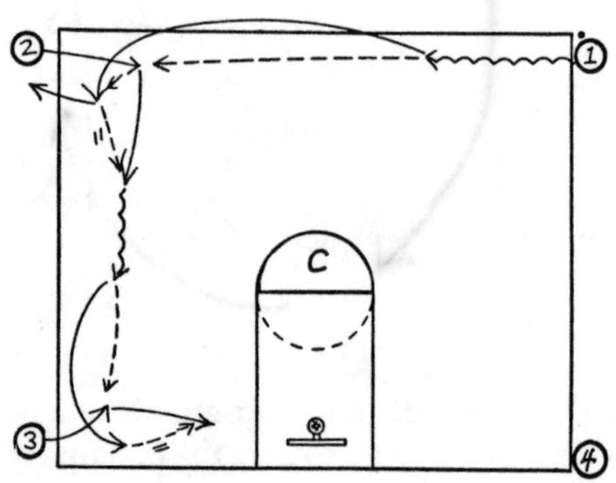

Directions: Divide the team into four groups. Have each group line up in one of the four corners. O1 starts the drill by dribbling the ball toward O2. O2 breaks toward O1 as O1 approaches. O2 should use a jump stop to meet the pass from O1. As soon as O1 passes to O2 he goes behind O2 for a handoff. O2 hands the ball to O1 and takes off toward O3. O1 then passes the ball back to O2, using a different pass and the drill continues between O2 and O3. The players need to remain out of bounds until the dribbler approaches so that the timing is right. You can add an additional basketball after a few minutes.

COACH ALLEN CORDER, ASSISTANT COACH—COLLEGE OF IDAHO

Coach Corder has been coaching for two years at the college level. While an assistant at the College of Idaho his teams have won 44 and lost only 14.

FOUR CORNER PASSING DRILL

Purpose: To develop good hands for passing and receiving the ball
Personnel and Equipment Needed: A minimum of ten players, one basketball and half the floor
Teaching Points: 1) Come out with a good target using your hands. 2) Snap the ball to the next player. 3) Do not bring the ball all the way back to your chest to pass. 4) Sprint to the end of the lines.
Directions: Divide the team into four groups. Have each of the groups line up in one of the corners. Then have them come toward each other until they are 12–15 feet apart. The ball is passed across to the player opposite, and then he passes to the player to his right. He then passes to the player across or opposite him, and that player passes the ball to the player to his right. Notice that in the diagram O1 starts with the ball. He passes the ball to O3. O3 then passes it to O4. O4 passes the ball to O2. O2 will then pass to O7. O7 passes to O5. O5 will pass to O6. O6 passes the ball to O8. O8 will pass to O9. Each player follows his pass and goes to the end of the line he passed to. This drill should be run for a minimum of two minutes. You should get a minimum of one hundred

forty-five passes. The ball should not touch the floor. If it does, stop the drill and have the players run a sprint or suicide, then start the drill over.

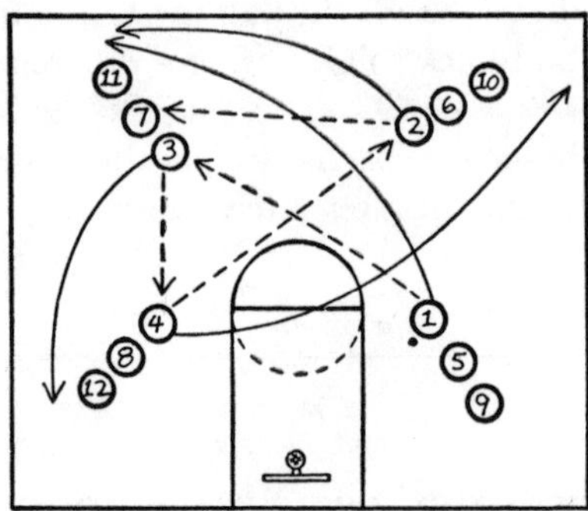

COACH CLIFF GARRISON—HENDRIX COLLEGE

Coach Garrison has been coaching for twenty-one years. Twelve of those twenty-one have been at the college level. He has a won/lost record of 195 wins and 112 losses at Hendrik College and 314 wins and 188 losses overall. His teams won the Arkansas Intercollegiate Conference in 1980 and 1981. He was named NAIA District 17 Coach of the Year in 1975 and 1980 and Arkansas Intercollegiate Conference Coach of the Year in 1980 and 1981.

SPLIT THE POST DRILL

Purpose: To improve passing, timing and cutting
Personnel and Equipment Needed: A minimum of five players, one basketball and a basket
Teaching Points: 1) Make sharp, crisp passes. 2) Catch the ball on the move. 3) Concentrate on the lay-up.
Directions: Have the five players align themselves as shown. O1 has the ball and can pass to O5 or to O2, who can pass to O5. Whoever hits the post splits first (if O1 passes to O5 he cuts by the post first and O2 cuts right off O1's cut). While the guards are making their cuts, the forwards (O3 and O4) move out to the guard positions. O5 passes the ball to either O3 or O4. O3 or O4 then passes to O5 and they make their

scissors cut off the post. O1 and O2 move back out to the guard positions and 05 passes the ball back out to one of them. They execute the third split off the post and this time O5 hands the ball off to one of them for the lay-up or shoots the ball himself. At this point you can have a new center come out with a ball, have O3 and O4 take the guard positions and O1 and O2 take the forward positions. Execute three more splits and a lay-up or jumper and then change not only the center, but also the guards and forwards.

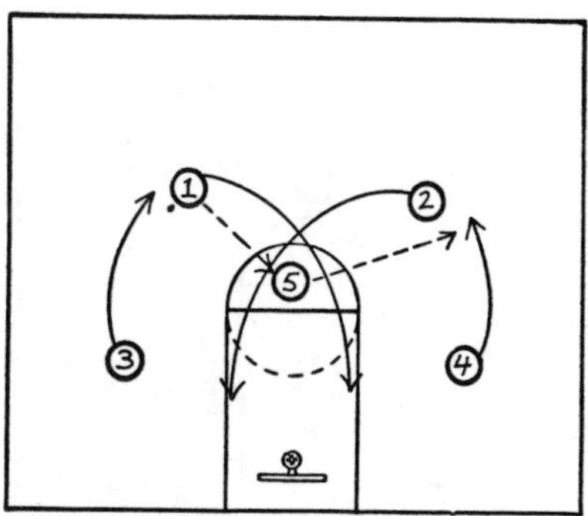

COACH BUTCH ESTES—PRESBYTERIAN COLLEGE

Coach Estes has been coaching for twelve years, all at the college level. He has been an assistant at Rice University, East Carolina University, and The Citadel. He took over a sagging program at Presbyterian College and has improved its won/lost record each year. His won/lost record at Presbyterian now stands at 42 wins and 41 losses.

FOUR MAN POST PASSING DRILL

Purpose: To teach passing into the low post
Personnel and Equipment Needed: A coach, a minimum of four players, one basketball and a basket
Teaching Points: 1) Low post should pin the defensive man's arm up. 2) The passer fakes a pass up and then uses a bounce pass to the post away from the defense.
Directions: Have four players align themselves as diagrammed. O1 has the ball and begins the drill by dribbling the ball to the right wing.

X2 plays defense on him. O4 posts up on that side and X3 comes over and plays defense on him. The ball is passed into O4 who tries to score on X3. After O4 scores, he throws the ball back to O1 who returns to the top of the key. He then dribbles to the left with X2 still guarding him. X3 now posts up and O4 comes across to guard him. Continue this procedure for 30 seconds. The coach then blows the whistle and each player rotates one position. You can have a group of four players at each basket.

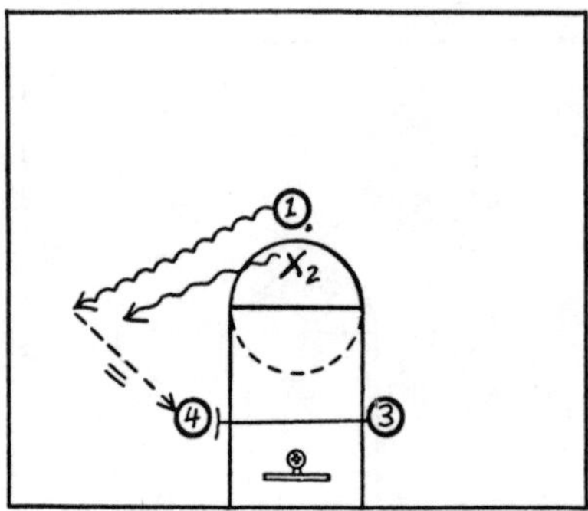

COACH RON MIKELS—GREENSBORO COLLEGE

Coach Mikels has been coaching for five years all at the college level. He was hired as a head coach in 1979 at the age of 24, making him one of the youngest head coaches in the nation. His 1982 team won the Washington and Lee Tournament by upsetting a strong Washington and Lee team. His 1983 team finished second in the Dixie Intercollegiate Athletic Conference with a 16–11 record.

PASS AND CATCH DRILL

Purpose: To improve passing and catching techniques
Personnel and Equipment Needed: An entire team of players, two basketballs and the entire floor
Teaching Points: 1) Make good passes. 2) Do not let the ball touch the floor. 3) Catch and pass the ball with the finger tips, not the palms.
Directions: Space six players along one side of the court as shown in the diagram. Line the rest of the team up behind the end line. O7 begins the drill by passing to O1. O1 passes the ball back to O7 and

goes to the end of the line behind O9. O7 then passes the ball to O2. O2 passes it back to O7 and replaces O1. O7 passes to O3. O3 makes a return pass to O7 and replaces O2. O7 passes to O4. O4 passes the ball back to O7 and replaces O3. O7 passes the ball to O5. O5 returns the ball to O7 and replaces O4. O7 then passes to O6. O6 passes back to O7 and replaces O5. O7 takes a jump shot, rebounds the ball, rolls it to the other end and replaces O6. The next player in line goes as soon as O7 takes his jumper. You can work on all three passes (chest, bounce and overhead) with this drill. The drill continues until everyone has been the shooter three times.

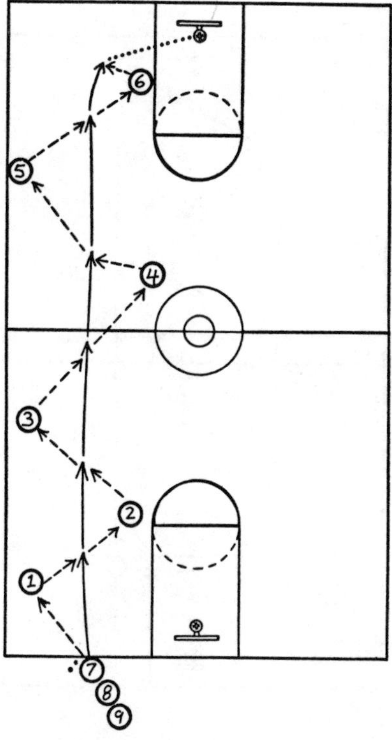

COACH JOHN W. McDOUGAL—NORTHERN ILLINOIS UNIVERSITY

Coach McDougal has been coaching for thirty-four years. Eight of those thirty-four have been at the college level. He has an overall won/lost record of 578 wins and 301 losses. His teams won the Mid-

American Conference in 1981 and 1982. He was named Mid-American Coach of the Year and Illinois Division I Coach of the Year in 1977.

NO FAULT SPEED DRILL

Purpose: To learn to handle the ball at an accelerated tempo without making turnovers
Personnel and Equipment Needed: An entire team of players, two basketballs and the entire floor
Teaching Points: 1) Execute good crisp passes. 2) Limit the dribbling.

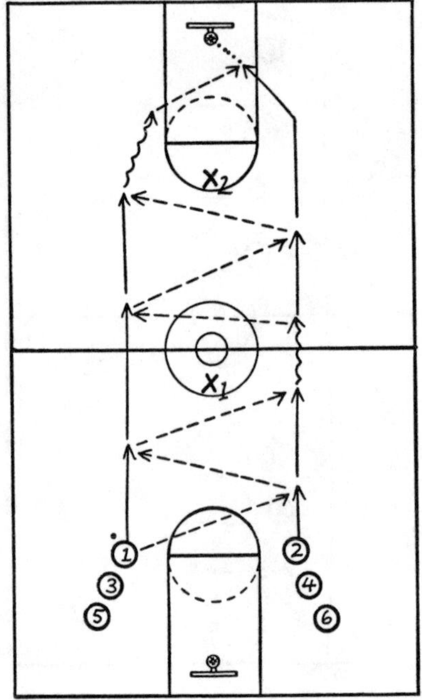

Directions: Have two players go out on defense (X1 and X2) to the center circle and the jump circle at the far end. The rest of the team forms two lines at the free throw line extended. The drill begins with the first player in each line (O1 and O2) passing the ball back and forth as they advance down the floor to the other end. Neither defensive man may leave his area (respective circle) but he tries to force the offense to pass or pick up the ball. The offensive players can not dribble except when the defender prevents a pass to his teammate. No offensive player may dribble more than two bounces without passing.

If a basket is scored without a turnover, the defenders remain on defense for the next two offensive players in line. The offense goes to the end of the line. If a mistake is made—bad pass, dribble, traveling, charge, or a missed lay-up—the offender goes on defense in place of one already in that position (whoever has been on defense the longest). The drill should be executed at full speed to simulate a game situation.

COACH TOM McCRACKEN—SOUTHERN UTAH STATE COLLEGE

Coach McCracken has been coaching for eighteen years. Five of those eighteen have been at the college level. He has a won/lost record of 50 wins and 30 losses at Southern Utah State and 286 wins and 119 losses overall. His team won the Heart of America Conference and he was named Heart of America Conference Coach of the Year.

THUNDERBIRD PASSING DRILL

Purpose: To improve the skills necessary to pass and catch the ball at full speed

Personnel and Equipment Needed: An entire team of players, two basketballs and the entire floor

Teaching Points: 1) Pass the ball out in front of the man. 2) Catch the ball with the finger tips, not the palms. 3) Pass and move quickly to the next spot.

Directions: Place five players on the floor as diagrammed. The rest of the team lines up behind the end line. O6 and O7 have basketballs. O6 begins the drill by passing the ball to O5 and running down the court at full speed. O5 passes the ball back to O6 and goes to the end of the line. O6 passes the ball to O4. O4 passes the ball back to O6 and replaces O5. O6 then passes to O2. O2 gives him a return pass for the lay-up and moves to replace O3. O6 shoots the lay-up and will become the next rebounder by replacing 01. 01 rebounds the ball and outlets it to O3 and then replaces O2. O3 throws a baseball pass to O8 and replaces O4. O7 continues the drill as soon as O6 has shot his lay-up. There should be no dribbling in this drill.

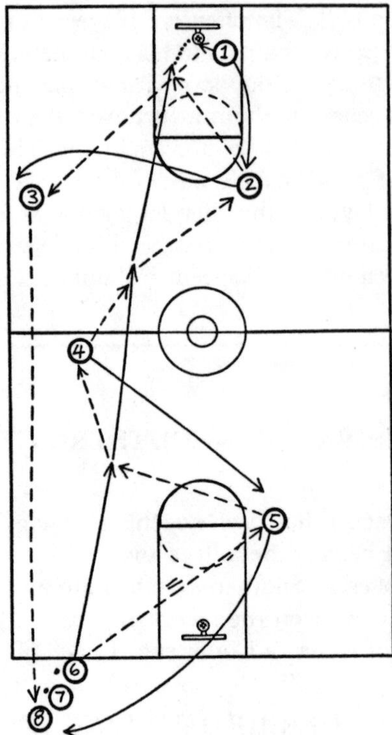

COACH DICK LIEN—UNIVERSITY OF WISCONSIN AT GREEN BAY

Coach Lien has been coaching for seventeen years. Four of those seventeen have been at the college level. He has an overall won/lost record at the college level of 79 wins and 36 losses.

EIGHT TIMES TWO PASSING DRILL

Purpose: To improve passing under pressure
Personnel and Equipment Needed: A minimum of ten players, one basketball and the entire floor
Teaching Points: 1) Make good snappy passes. 2) Hit the open man. 3) Protect the ball in the double team. 4) Defense must double-team in their zone.

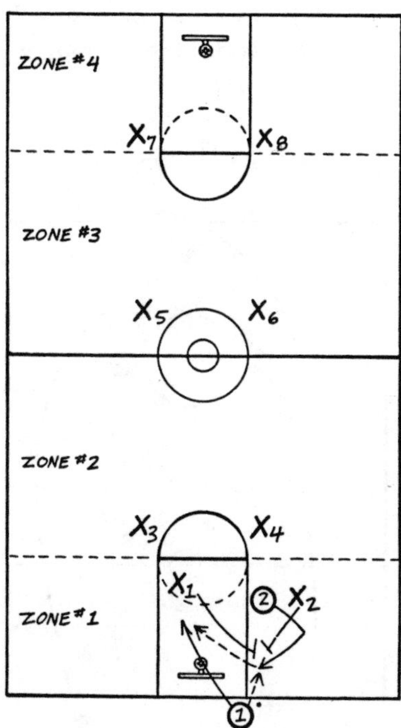

Directions: O1 and O2 must bring the ball up the floor via the pass only against eight defensive players (two in each of the four zones as shown). The key to this drill is to have the defense double-team the ball and not play it soft. The drill culminates with O1 and O2 scoring a lay-up. The rotation is to have each pair move up to the next zone with O1 and O2 taking zone four.

COACH JIM BOYLE—ST. JOSEPH'S UNIVERSITY

Coach Boyle has been in college coaching for two years. He has a won/lost record of 40 wins and 18 losses at St. Joseph's University. He was named NABC District III, Division I, Coach of the Year in 1982.

FOUR-MINUTE PASSING DRILL

Purpose: To improve passing and catching skills and concentration
Personnel and Equipment Needed: An entire team of players, two basketballs, a clock and the entire floor

Teaching Points: 1) Make good snappy passes. 2) Catch the ball with finger tips, not palms. 3) Do not dribble the ball at all. 4) Do not let the ball touch the floor.

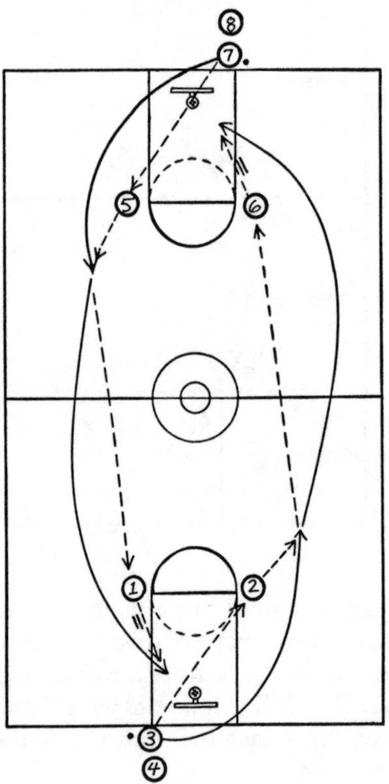

Directions: Divide the team into two lines, one at each end of the floor under the basket. Have the first two players in each line position themselves at the elbows (O1, O2, O5 and O6). Set the clock for four minutes. Balls are placed in each line. On the whistle, the first player in each line passes to the player at the right elbow. He then runs outside and receives a return pass. Upon receiving the return pass, he passes the ball to the player at the elbow at the other end. He follows his pass and receives a return bounce pass and goes in for a lay-up. He then goes to the end of the line and the next player in line takes the ball out of the net and continues the drill until the four minutes have elapsed. The team should be able to make about 90 lay-ups in four minutes.

COACH GARY BAYS—WARNER PACIFIC COLLEGE

Coach Bays has been coaching for nine years. Seven of those nine have been at the college level. His 1982–83 team finished with an impressive 24–9 record and won the National Christian College Athletic Association District 8 championship. He was named NCCAA District 8 Coach of the Year in 1983.

FULL COURT PASSING AND LAY-UP DRILL

Purpose: To encourage communication, good passing and making lay-ups
Personnel and Equipment Needed: A minimum of five players, one basketball and the entire floor
Teaching Points: 1) The ball must not hit the floor. 2) The players must call out their positions. 3) Concentrate and make good passes.

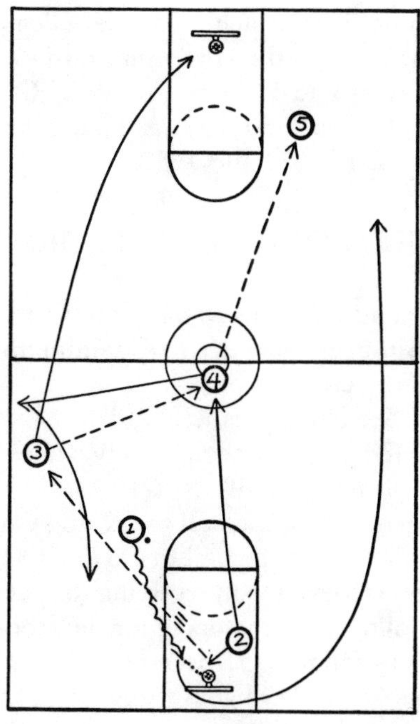

Directions: Have five players assume the positions shown (O1–O5). The drill begins with O1 dribbling in and shooting a lay-up. He then crosses under the basket and sprints to the other end to become an outlet. O2, the rebounder, grabs the ball out of the net and passes it to O3, the outlet. He then proceeds to the middle. O3 passes the ball to O4, the middle, and runs to the other end to rebound. O4 passes to the shooter at the other end (O5) and sprints to the sideline away from the ball to the opposite end to become the next shooter. The drill continues in this fashion with the following rotation: the shooter becomes the outlet, the outlet becomes the rebounder, the rebounder becomes the middle, the middle becomes the shooter. To involve the entire team, simply place extra people at the designated spots and replace the shooter each time. Run this drill for a designated amount of time (three–five minutes) and set goals for the number of lay-ups during that time, for example, 40 lay-ups in three minutes.

COACH LYLE DAMON—SAN FRANCISCO STATE UNIVERSITY

Coach Damon has been coaching at the collegiate level for eleven years. He has a won/lost record of 134 wins and 143 losses at San Francisco State and 337 wins and 177 losses overall. His team won the Far Western Conference title in 1980. He was named Far Western Conference Coach of the Year in 1973 and 1980.

FULL COURT DETAIL DRILL

Purpose: To teach and emphasize ball handling details
Personnel and Equipment Needed: A minimum of seven players, two basketballs and the entire floor
Teaching Points: See Directions.
Directions: Have the players line up into two lines at opposite ends of the floor, with two players at half-court. O1 and O4 have basketballs and start the drill by outleting the ball to O2 and O5. They dribble the ball across half-court and pass the ball to O3 and O6 and then cut hard to the basket for a return pass. Upon receiving the pass back they make a lay-up. O3 and O6 follow the shooters in for the rebound and outlet the ball. The rotation is as follows: O1 becomes O2, O2 goes to the end of the line, O4 becomes O5 and O5 goes to the end of the line.

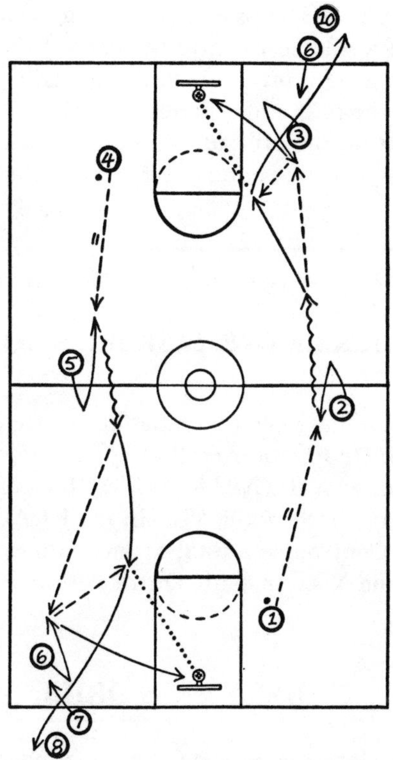

Emphasis:

Mid-court men (02 and 05)

1) Wait for eye contact.
2) Then step away.
3) Give target (hand).
4) Come to meet the pass as it is being thrown.
5) Upon reception, pivot to the side position away from the pressure.
6) Then begin a dribble without traveling.
7) Then stop (do not pass off the move).
8) Pass the ball to the corner and cut hard.
9) The lay-up must be off the glass and soft.

Corner men (03 and 06)

1) Wait for eye contact.
2) Then step away.
3) Give a target (hand).

4) Come to meet the pass as it is being thrown.
5) Assume a side position (to the basket).
6) Make a good return pass to the cutter.
7) Follow the pass and rebound the ball.
8) Bust out on the dribble.
9) Make a good two-hand overhead outlet pass.

COACH JOHN HICKMAN—PITTSBURG STATE UNIVERSITY

Coach Hickman has been coaching for nineteen years, all of them at the college level. He has an overall won/lost record of 265 wins and 243 losses. His team won the NAIA District 16 championship in 1975. He has been named Coach of the Year in the KCAC, MCAU and the Heart of America Conference a total of seven times. He has also been named Coach of the Year in both District 16 and District 10 of the NAIA.

TWENTY PASS DRILL

Purpose: To develop passing, catching, pivoting and screening skills
Personnel and Equipment Needed: A minimum of eight players, one basketball and a basket
Teaching Points: 1) Come to meet the pass. 2) Do not pass the ball to a man going away. 3) Catch the ball with the finger tips, not the palms.

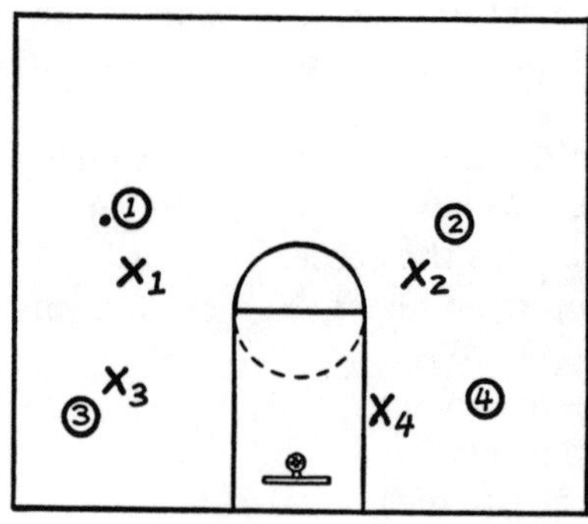

Directions: Divide the team into four-on-four teams. Put one team of four on offense and one team of four on defense. The offense must follow these rules: 1) Always pass the ball. 2) Do not dribble. The defense can not double-team, trap, switch, or jump and rotate. The offense must make 20 passes in 45 seconds. If the offense scores a basket, it counts as three passes and you restart the clock from the point and time of the basket. If the defense fouls, you add three passes to the offense. If the offense fumbles the ball, dribbles it, gets a five-second count, even if the defense just deflects it, for any violation the offense loses. The losers run a set of lines. Go three times and then switch the offense and defense.

Part II

CONDITIONING DRILLS

COACH DAN A. CARNEVALE—CALIFORNIA STATE POLYTECHNIC UNIVERSITY AT POMONA

Coach Carnevale has been coaching for fourteen years. Twelve of those fourteen have been at the college level as either an assistant or a head coach. He has been an assistant at Colorado State University and under Tex Winter at Long Beach State University. Coach Carnevale's outside credentials include a short period when he was the technical director of the movie and television series "The White Shadow." Prior to that, he provided the same expertise for the film "One On One" and choreographed all the basketball sequences.

INS AND OUTS DRILL

Purpose: To improve a player's condition
Personnel and Equipment Needed: A minimum of one player and a maximum of an entire team of players and the entire floor
Teaching Points: 1) Make sure the players keep a 15- to 18-foot spacing between each other. 2) Use in conjunction with other conditioning drills
Directions: This drill utilizes the whole gymnasium. O1 starts at one wall at the end of the court. He jogs from the wall to a point approximately halfway between the wall and the baseline. At that point he explodes into a full stride until he reaches the top of the free throw circle. He quickly changes his tempo back to a jog and jogs to the top of the free throw circle at the far end of the floor. Again, he explodes into full stride to a point halfway between the baseline and the wall. He will then jog from that point to the wall, turn right and jog along the wall to a point on the other side of the free throw lane as shown. He then turns right again and heads down the floor, still jogging till he reaches that point halfway between the wall and the baseline. He repeats the ins and outs until he reaches his original starting point. He should do ten repetitions around the gym and rest for 30 seconds between each repetition.

Note: If you are conditioning your entire team, just divide the squad in half and station them at opposite corners of the gym. Have them run clockwise, so that at each end of the gym (wall) they will get a few seconds of time for recovery before continuing the next leg of the drill.

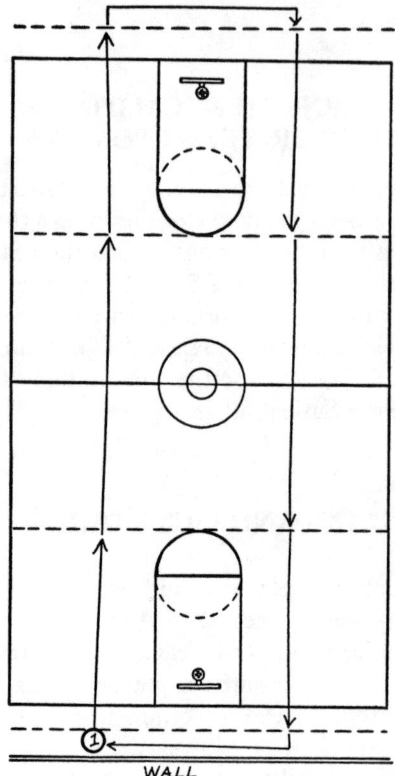

COACH BILL WILLIAMS—STATE UNIVERSITY OF NEW YORK AT CORTLAND

Coach Williams has been coaching for fourteen years. Two of those fourteen have been at the college level. He has a won/lost record at S.U.N.Y. at Cortland of 31 wins and 17 losses.

TIGHT GAME CONDITIONING DRILL

Purpose: To improve conditioning and execution of the offense and the defense when tired

Personnel and Equipment Needed: A minimum of ten players, one basketball, a scoreclock and the entire floor
Teaching Points: 1) Stress what you want to work on in the last minute (free throw shooting, pressing—man-to-man or zone, working against the press—man-to-man or zone, or the delay game).

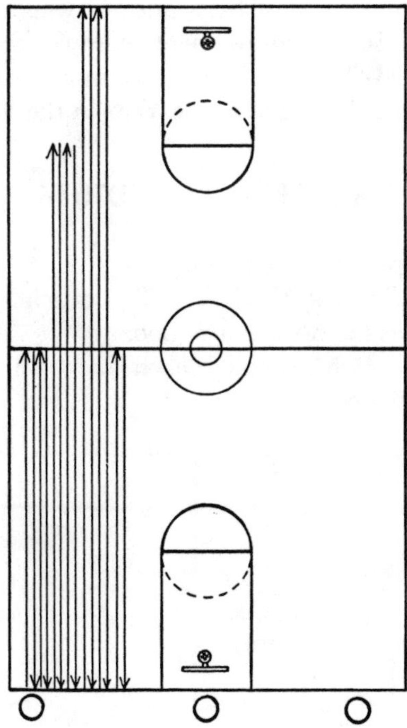

Directions: Have your players run the standard suicide drill for one minute (twice to half-court and back, twice to three-quarters court and back, twice from baseline to baseline and back and then once to half-court and back again timed).

With one minute on the clock you should start a scrimmage immediately after the suicide. Make the score close, simulating the end of a tight game. Fouls are called and shot. Timeouts are not called, so the players must know your last-minute strategy. You should press and work against the press in this drill. The team that ends up with the loss runs again (just for fun).

COACH GEORGE L. BIANCHI—ARMSTRONG STATE COLLEGE

Coach Bianchi has been coaching for thirteen years. Eight of those thirteen have been at the college level. He has a won/lost record of 84 wins and 52 losses at Armstrong State and 161 wins and 94 losses overall. His teams have won several tournament championships at both the high school and college levels. He was named National Association of Basketball Coaches Division II Coach of the Year in the South in 1979.

SIXTEEN LINE DRILL

Purpose: To improve conditioning
Personnel and Equipment Needed: Two coaches, two managers, an entire team of players and the entire floor
Teaching Points: 1) Must touch each line with your foot. 2) Must touch 16 lines in 60 seconds.

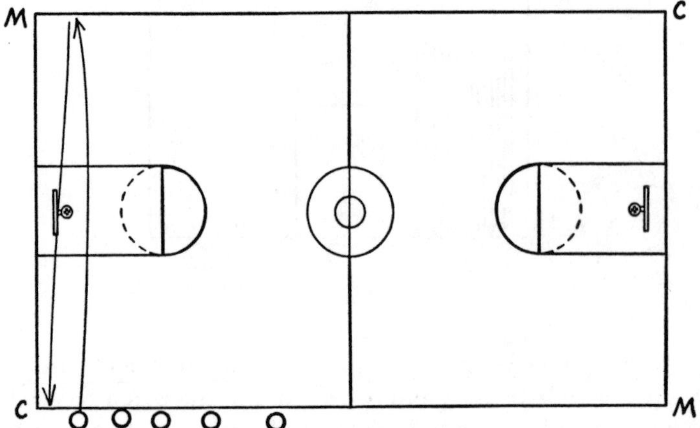

Directions: Position the two coaches and two managers (as shown) in the four corners. Then have the entire team line up along the sideline with both feet behind the sideline. On the whistle, the players must run across the floor and touch the opposite sideline with their feet and then return to the sideline they started at and touch it. They repeat this procedure as many times as they can within 60 seconds. They must touch every line with their feet and touch a minimum of 16 lines or they have to do it again.

COACH CHARLES TRAFTON—OAKLAND CITY COLLEGE

Coach Trafton has been coaching for sixteen years. Ten of those sixteen have been at the college level. He has an overall won/lost record of 230 wins and 172 losses. His teams have finished third in 1978, second in 1980 and 1982 and won the National Little College Athletic Association title in 1981. He was also named NLCAA Tournament Coach of the Year in 1981.

MAZE DRILL

Purpose: To improve the players condition, quickness and ball handling

Personnel and Equipment Needed: Twelve players, six basketballs and the entire floor

Teaching Points: 1) Slide as quickly as possible. 2) Explode on your jumps. 3) Dribble with both hands.

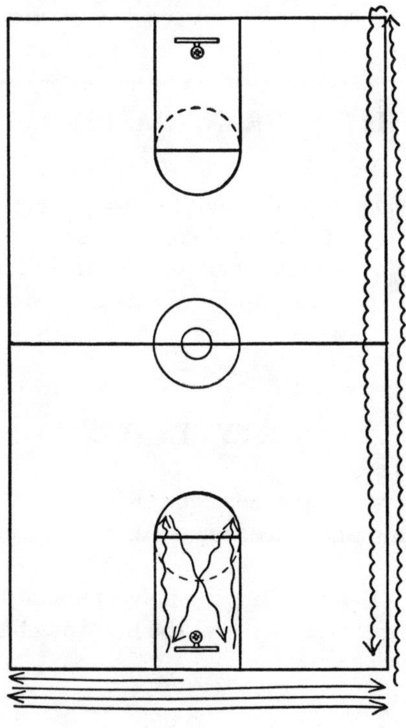

Directions: First divide the players into four groups of three each. Place groups one and two at one end of the floor and groups three and four at the other end. Group one and group three begin simultaneously at different ends of the floor.

1) They slide defensively around and through the free throw lane as diagrammed.
2) They do five jumps as high as possible.
3) Next, they do three and a half sprints from sideline to sideline.
4) Finally, they receive a ball and dribble down the court with their right hands and back with their left hands.

Groups two and four should start when groups one and three have begun their second sprint.

Note: Make sure that both groups one and three, and two and four start on the same side of the floor so that when the dribbling begins they are on opposite sidelines.

COACH ROGER HAUN—GRAND RAPIDS BAPTIST COLLEGE

Coach Haun has been coaching for twelve years all at the college level as either an assistant or a head coach. His teams at Grand Rapids Baptist College finished either first or second in the North Central Christian Athletic Conference all four years they were members.

"SIXTY" DRILL

Purpose: To improve a player's condition
Personnel and Equipment Needed: An entire team of players and the entire floor
Teaching Points: 1) Make sure the players touch the lines with their feet. 2) Run in straight lines—stop at the line and change direction. Do not round off the corners.

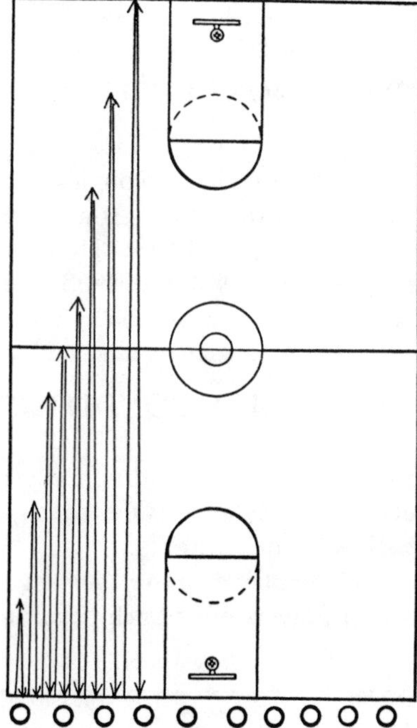

Directions: Have the players line up behind the baseline. On the whistle they sprint to the bottom of the first jump circle, touch that line with their feet, change direction and come back and touch the baseline. After they touch the baseline, they change direction again and run back to the top of the first jump circle. They touch the line with their feet, change direction and go back and touch the baseline. After touching the baseline, they change direction and sprint to the bottom of the next jump circle which they touch and sprint back to the baseline. They touch the baseline and sprint back to the half-court line, touch it and return to the baseline. They again touch the baseline and then sprint to the top of the second jump circle and return to the baseline. After touching the baseline, they sprint to the bottom of the next jump circle touch the line and return to the baseline. Then they touch the baseline and sprint back to the top of the third jump circle and back to the baseline. After touching the baseline, they sprint to the other baseline touch it and sprint back. They should accomplish this in 60 seconds.

COACH PAT KENNEDY—IONA COLLEGE

Coach Kennedy has been coaching for eleven years all at the college level. In four years at Iona he has a won/lost record of 83 wins and 40 losses. His teams have won the Metro Atlantic Athletic Conference and the Manufacturer's Hanover Classic. He was a finalist for the MAAC Coach of the Year in 1982 and 1983 and a finalist for the Widmer Cup Poll Coach of the Year in 1982.

THREE-MAN DEFENSIVE CONDITIONING DRILL

Purpose: To improve the players' condition and reaction to the ball
Personnel and Equipment Needed: One coach, an entire team of players, two basketballs and the entire floor.
Teaching Points: 1) Have players move their legs quickly. 2) Players must react to the ball. 3) Players must back-pedal into the key area.

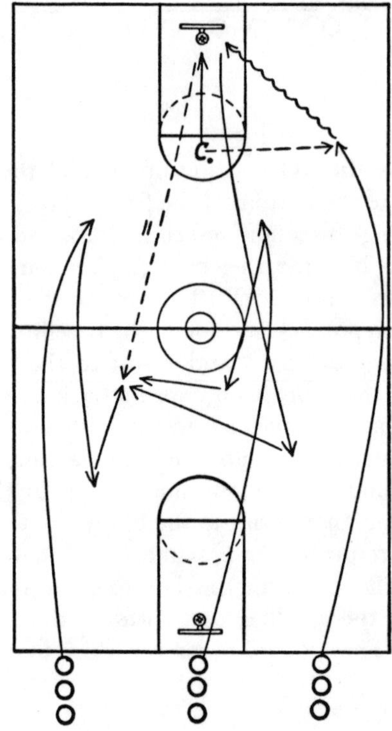

Directions: Have the players form three lines on the baseline and the coach position himself on the opposite free throw line. The drill starts with the first player in each line sprinting down the floor toward the coach. As they approach, the coach passes the ball to (any) one of them and they take a hard driving lay-up. The coach rebounds the ball out of the net. As he does so, the three players back-pedal as hard as they can back into the defensive key area. The coach then throws a two-handed overhead pass to an area on the court, the players converge, and get the loose ball. They step off the floor and the next player in each line continues the drill. The drill continues until all the players have gone three times.

COACH JIM KLEIN—STATE UNIVERSITY OF NEW YORK COLLEGE OF TECHNOLOGY

Coach Klein has been coaching for twenty-five years. Two of those twenty-five have been at the college level. He has an overall won/lost record of 318 wins and 76 losses. Coach Klein has also coached in the professional ranks in the C.B.A.

FULL COURT DRILL

Purpose: To improve conditioning, following your shots and ball handling

Personnel and Equipment Needed: A minimum of twelve players, two basketballs and the entire floor

Teaching Points: 1) Move the ball up the court quickly. 2) See the court before you dribble. 3) Shoot and follow your shot for the rebound. 4) Faking down the floor and coming back to meet the pass.

Directions: Have the players line up in pairs at each baseline and on both sides of the court at the free throw line extended as shown. The ball starts out of bounds with O1 and is passed to O2 at the free throw line extended (O2 should fake down court and come back to meet the ball). O2 catches the ball (with his back to the sideline) and looks up the court before putting the ball on the floor. He then dribbles twice up the sideline and hits O3 with a pass at the other free throw line extended (O3 should also fake down court and come back to meet the pass). O3 then dribbles the ball toward the basket and pulls up to take a 12-foot jumper. He follows his shot, rebounds it and passes it to O10 who continues the drill up the other sideline. The rotation of players is as follows:

O1 goes to the end of O2's line, O2 goes to the end of O3's line and O3 goes to the end of O4's line. Begin this drill with two balls, one at each baseline. You can add more balls as the drill progresses.

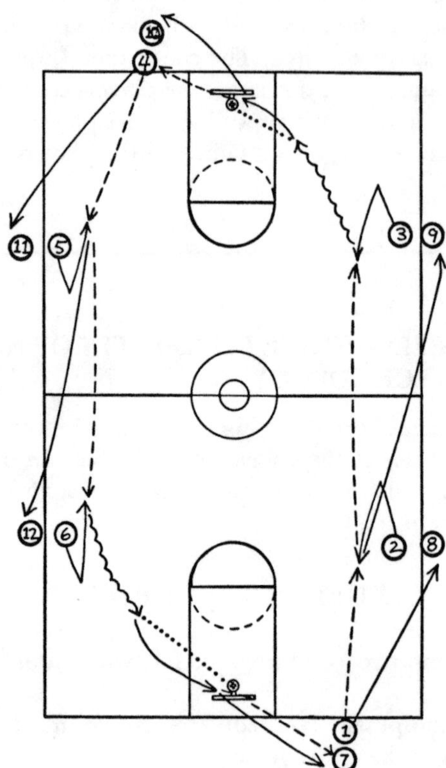

COACH MAC PETTY—WABASH COLLEGE

Coach Petty has been coaching for fifteen years. Twelve of those fifteen have been at the college level. He has a won/lost record of 106 wins and 66 losses at Wabash and 154 wins and 94 losses overall. His team won the NCAA Division III national championship in 1982. He was named the Kodak Coach of the Year for Division III of the NCAA in 1982.

PINWHEEL DRILL

Purpose: To improve a player's condition, passing and catching skills and lay-up technique
Personnel and Equipment Needed: A minimum of ten players, two basketballs and the entire floor
Teaching Points: 1) Make good passes, leading the man on the move. 2) Concentrate on the lay-ups. 3) Can create competition by having the players make so many baskets in so many minutes.

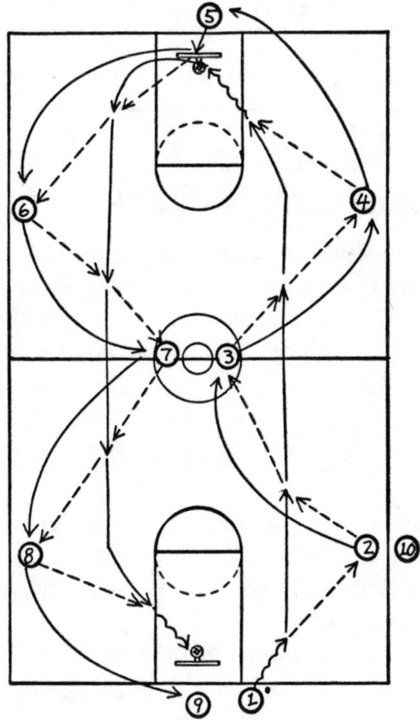

Directions: Position the players as shown. O1 begins with the ball and passes it to O2; O2 returns the ball to O1 who then passes it to O3. O2, after passing the ball to O1, moves to take the place of O3. O3 passes the ball back to O1 who then passes it to O4. O3, after passing the ball back to O1, moves to replace O4. O4 passes the ball back to O1 who takes it in for a lay-up. After O4 passes to O1 he goes to take the place of

O5. O5 rebounds O1's lay-up and passes the ball to O1. O5 then advances to O6's spot. O1 passes the ball to O6 and continues down the floor for a return pass. O6 passes the ball back to O1 who then passes it to O7. O6 after passing the ball back to O1 moves to replace O7. O7 passes the ball back to O1 who then passes it to O8. O7, after passing the ball back to O1, takes the place of O8. O8 passes the ball back to O1 who takes it in for a lay-up. O8 rebounds O1's lay-up and goes behind O9. O1, after shooting the second lay-up goes behind O10. As soon as O1 lays the ball in, O9 begins by passing to O10 and the drill continues.

Note: If you have more than ten players they line up behind O10.

Variation: It is possible to have two balls going at the same time.

COACH GENE SMITHSON—WICHITA STATE UNIVERSITY

Coach Smithson has been coaching at the college level for twelve years. He has a won/lost record of 80 wins and 39 losses at Wichita State and 146 wins and 57 losses overall. His team won the Missouri Valley Conference championship and went to the NCAA Mid-West Regional finals in 1981.

FULL COURT PITCH PASS DRILL

Purpose: To improve a player's condition, passing, and transition abilities.
Personnel and Equipment Needed: A minimum of two players, one basketball and the entire floor
Teaching Points: 1) Drill must be done at full speed. 2) You can use two different passes—overhead two-hand pitch pass and the baseball pass.
Directions: Have the players line up in two lines on either side of the free throw lanes as shown. The ball starts with O1. O2 breaks for the opposite basket. O1 pitches the ball on the fly to the breaking player (O2) who should catch the ball somewhere between the half-court line and the top of the free throw circle. O2 continues at full speed for a lay-up. After O1 pitches the ball he takes off at full speed toward the other end. He must rebound O2's lay-up before it hits the ground. O2, after his lay-up, takes off back toward the original end. O1 turns and pitches the rebound to O2 and takes off to catch O2's rebound at the original

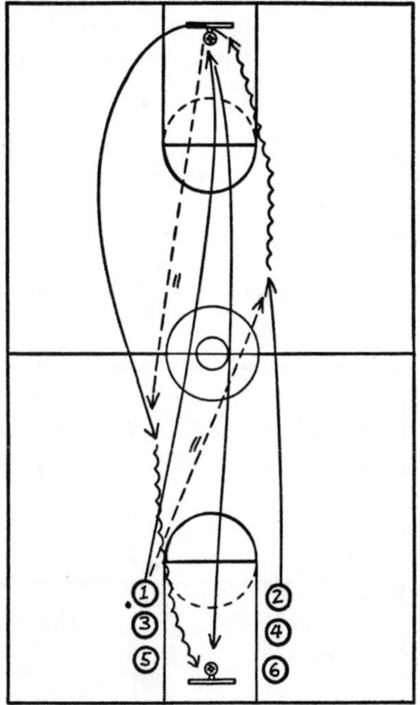

end. If either the lay-up is missed or the ball hits the floor after the lay-up, the same two players must go again. After the two players successfully complete the drill they switch lines.

COACH JIM CONNOR—THOMAS MORE COLLEGE

Coach Jim Connor has been coaching for thirty-four years. Ten of those thirty-four have been at the college level. He has a won/lost record of 514 wins and 227 losses. His teams have won several championships over the years. He was named NAIA District 32 Coach of the Year in 1981.

TWO MAN FULL COURT LAY-UP DRILL

Purpose: To improve conditioning, ball handling and lay-ups
Personnel and Equipment Needed: A minimum of four players, two basketballs and the entire floor

Teaching Points: 1) Use crisp passes to advance the ball down the floor. 2) Get the lay-up high on the board. 3) Go at full speed the entire time.

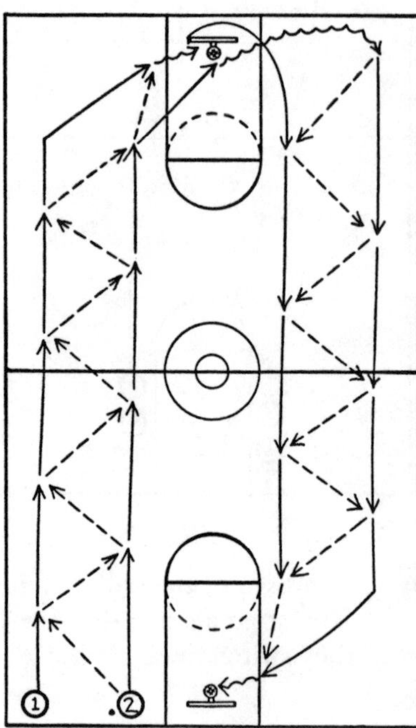

Directions: Have the players line up in two lines on the left-hand side of the floor as shown. O1 and O2 pass the ball back and forth as they sprint down the floor on the left-hand side. O2 stops at the free throw line, takes the ball away from O1 as though he is going to drive and then plants his outside foot and brings the ball back on a pass to O1. O1 is the closest man to the sideline, and when he reaches the free throw line extended he angles toward the basket and receives the pass from O2 for the lay-up. O2 follows in to rebound the lay-up by O1. O2 then takes the outside position and O1 the inside position as they continue the drill by going down the other side of the floor. O3 and O4 begin when O1 and O2 have reached half-court on their initial trip down the floor. The drill can continue as long as you wish.

COACH RON PETRO—MARIST COLLEGE

Coach Petro has been coaching for twenty-one years. Nineteen of those twenty-one have been at the college level. In his career at Marist College his teams have compiled 231 victories. His team won the Central Athletic College Conference title in 1968–69. His 1970–71 team was a finalist at the NAIA National Tournament and his 1972–73 team was the NAIA Regional champion.

FIVE-MINUTE LAY-UP DRILL

Purpose: To improve conditioning, concentration and reaching a goal

Personnel and Equipment Needed: Two managers, a minimum of ten players, three basketballs and the entire floor

Teaching Points: 1)Use a two-handed chest pass. 2) Concentrate on the lay-up. 3) Make the goal attainable, but difficult.

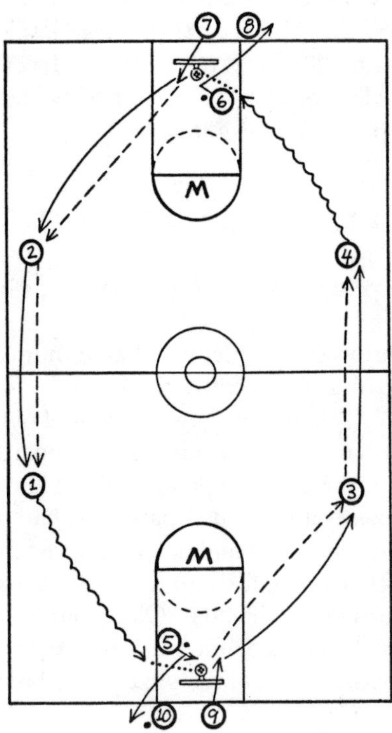

Directions: Position your players as diagrammed. The drill begins with O5 and O6 shooting lay-ups at opposite ends of the floor. O9 rebounds O5's lay-up and O7 rebounds O6's lay-up. O5 and O6 go to the ends of the lines behind O10 and O8. O9 passes the ball to O3 and O7 passes the ball to O2 and then they replace the men they passed to. O3 passes the ball to O4 and O2 passes his ball to O1. They (O3 and O2) also replace the men they passed to. O4 and O1 dribble the ball in for the lay-up and go to the end of the line and the drill continues. O10 has the third ball and he puts it into play as soon as O9 has replaced O3. The goal should be around 170 lay-ups in five minutes. The managers positioned at the free throw lines count. If the goal is not reached, have the team run a punishment drill and then attempt the five-minute lay-up drill again. You can also have the players work on their left-hand lay-ups by reversing the direction of the drill.

DR. GLENN WILKES—STETSON UNIVERSITY

Coach Wilkes has been coaching for thirty-three years. Thirty-two of those thirty-three have been at the college level. He has a won/lost record of 413 wins and 289 losses at Stetson University. He has been recognized by the NABC for over 500 career wins and also been inducted into the Florida Sports Hall of Fame.

MANMAKER LAY-UP AND CONDITIONING DRILL

Purpose: To improve lay-ups at full speed, passing on the move and conditioning
Personnel and Equipment Needed: A minimum of three players, two cones, one basketball and the entire floor
Teaching Points: 1) Keep the passes high and in front of target. 2) Go at full speed. 3) Shoot the lay-up high on the board.
Directions: Have the players line up in three lines as shown. O2 starts with the ball and passes it to O1. O1 passes the ball back to O2 who then passes it to O3. O3 passes the ball back to O2 who passes it to O1 for the driving lay-up. After passing the ball to O1, O2 cuts around the cone in the corner and heads down the floor. O3 rebounds the ball and passes it to O1 who has cut up the sideline after his lay-up. O1 passes the ball back to O3 who passes it to O2 for the driving lay-up.

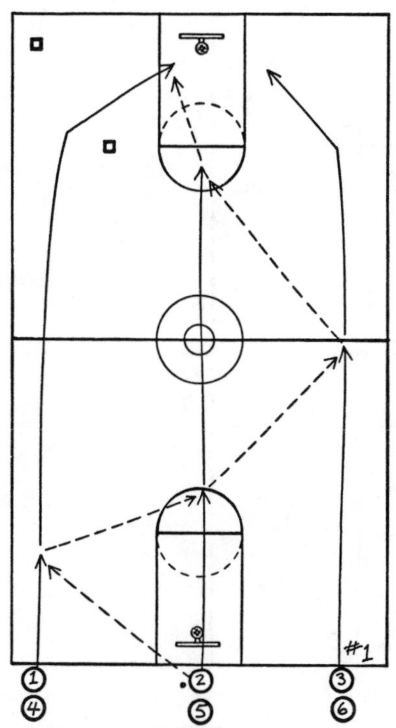

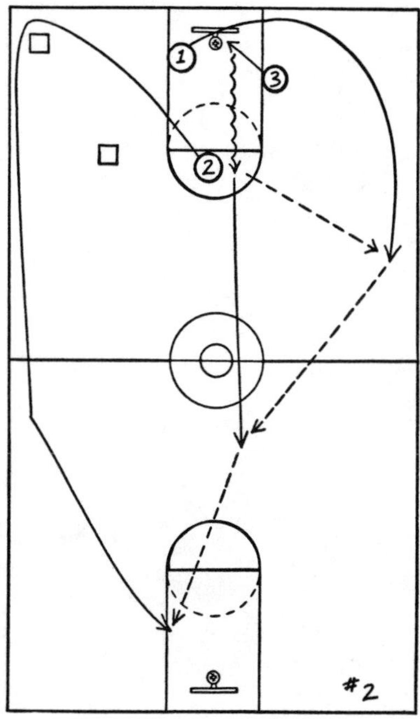

COACH JOHN D. HILL—HEIDELBERG COLLEGE

Coach Hill has been coaching for fifteen years. Seven of those fifteen have been at the college level. He has a collegiate won/lost record of 106 wins and 84 losses. His team won the Northern Division Tournament of the Ohio Athletic Conference in 1982.

FOUR-TEAM CONDITIONING DRILL

Purpose: To improve the players' condition at the end of practice instead of just running

Personnel and Equipment Needed: A minimum of twelve players, one basketball and the entire floor

Teaching Points: 1) Do not play sloppy. 2) Take only good shots. 3) Push yourself when you are tired.

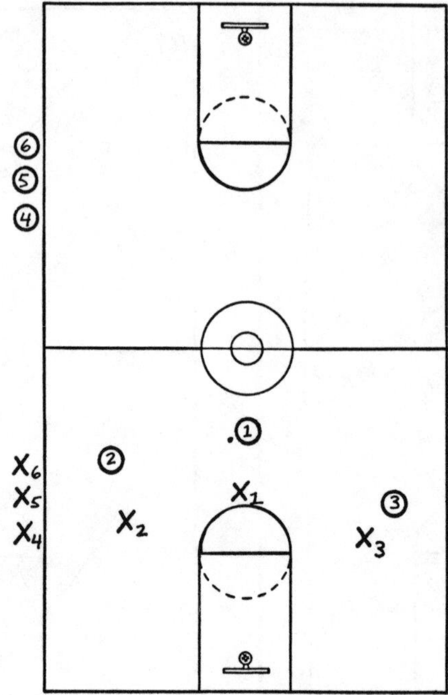

Directions: Divide the players into four teams of three each. Two of the four teams are on offense and two are on defense. They play three-on-three full court. When one team scores two baskets they are replaced by their subs who are waiting along the sideline. The team that is first scored upon twice must stay until they score three times, or have been scored upon four times, before their subs replace them. Both teams must fast-break and press man-to-man the entire time. The drill lasts for ten minutes.

Variation: You may go four-on-four instead of three-on-three.

COACH RANDY LAMBERT—MARYVILLE COLLEGE

Coach Lambert has been coaching for six years. Three of those six have been at the college level. He has an overall won/lost record of 76 wins and 54 losses.

SWEET SIXTEEN DRILL

Purpose: To improve a player's agility, quickness, reaction time and overall conditioning

Personnel and Equipment Needed: A minimum of two players and maximum of 32 players, rebounder, toss-back, bench, medicine or weighted ball, four jump ropes, a standard, a rope, a weight, a roll of tape, five basketballs and the entire floor

Teaching Points: 1) Begin with 30 seconds at each station. 2) Increase 10 seconds each week. 3) Make two complete trips through the stations for each workout.

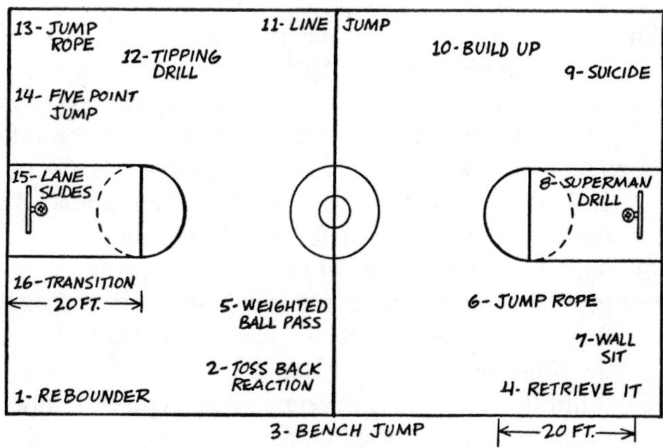

Directions: Set up the stations as diagrammed and described:

1) Rebounder—Pull the ball down and through the rebounding arm to your chest and repeat.
2) Toss-back reaction—One player (A) will face player (B) and be between player B and the toss-back. Player (B) will throw the ball off the toss-back and player (A) will pivot and catch the ball (the toss-back can be replaced with the wall).
3) Bench jump—A player will jump with his feet together back and forth across a two-foot-high bench.
4) Retrieve it—Lines are placed 20 feet apart on the floor with tape. Player (A) will have two balls and be 15 feet away

from player (B) facing him. Player (A) will roll the first ball to either line and player (B) will retrieve it and pass it back. While player (B) is retrieving the first ball, Player (A) will roll the second ball to the opposite line and as soon as player (B) passes the first ball back he goes after the second one. This continues for the 30-seconds interval.

5) Weighted ball pass—Players face each other 15 feet apart and execute various passes, using proper form with a weighted ball.
6) Jump rope—Both players will jump rope throughout the allotted time.
7) Wall sit—Both players will lower their butts and place their backs against the wall in a sitting position throughout the allotted time.
8) Superman drill—One player begins with a basketball and throws the ball off the backboard to the other side of the lane. Then he tries to catch the ball as high as possible and land with both feet outside of the lane on the other side. The player will then throw the ball back across the board and attempt to rebound it in the same manner. This continues from side to side for the 30 seconds.
9) Suicide—One player will run the lines: baseline to free throw line and back, baseline to half-court and back, baseline to the other free throw line and back, and baseline to the other baseline and back.
10) Build-up jump—Tie a weight to one end of a rope and tie the other end to a standard three feet off the floor. One player will begin at the weighted end and jump back and forth across the rope with his feet together, moving up the rope. Once he gets to the standard, he will come back in a similar manner and repeat for the 30 seconds.
11) Line jump—One player will jump back and forth across the sideline as quickly as possible, without touching the line.
12) Tipping—Player (A) will start with a ball on one side of the goal and player (B) will be on the other side. Player (A) will toss the ball against the backboard to the other side; player (B) will time his jump and tap the ball back to player A. This will be repeated for the allotted time.
13) Jump rope—Both players will jump rope throughout the allotted time.

14) Five-Point Jump—One player will jump to each point with his feet together for the allotted time.
15) Lane slides—One player, in defensive stance, will slide from one side of the free throw lane to the other, placing his hands outside of the lane.
16) Transition—A line is placed on the floor 20 feet from the baseline. One player will sprint to the line and run backwards back to the baseline. This is repeated for the entire 30 seconds.

Part III

DEFENSIVE DRILLS

COACH HOMER DREW—BETHEL COLLEGE

Coach Drew has been coaching for sixteen years. Thirteen of those sixteen have been at the college level. He has a won/lost record of 166 wins and 64 losses at Bethel and 199 wins and 104 losses overall. His teams have won the National Christian College Athletic Association District III championships five consecutive years. He was selected NCCAA District Coach of the Year in 1978, 1980, 1981 and 1982 and NCCAA National Coach of the Year in 1980.

REACTION DRILL

Purpose: To improve players' defensive reaction
Personnel and Equipment Needed: The entire team, two managers and/or coaches, two basketballs and the entire floor
Teaching Points: 1) Correct defensive stance. 2) Proper defensive slides. 3) Quickness in reaction. 4) Learn the floor won't hurt you. 5) Quick acceleration. 6) Keep body under control. 7) Fast break.
Directions: The coaches position themselves as diagrammed. The players divide themselves into three lines along the baseline. The drill begins with the first coach giving a hand signal for players X1, X2, X3 to come to the free throw line and stay alive with short, quick, stutter steps in defensive stance. Next the first coach gives one of the following hand signals:

1) Points left—X1, X2, X3 take two quick defensive slides to the left.
2) Points right—X1, X2, X3 take two quick defensive slides to the right.
3) Points back—X1, X2, X3 take two quick defensive slides back.
4) Points forward—X1, X2, X3 take two quick defensive slides forward.
5) Palms down—X1, X2, X3 hit the floor with their chests and pop right back up and continue stutter stepping in defensive stance.
6) Thumbs pointing down the court—X1, X2, X3 sprint to half-court and slow down, and get their bodies under control.

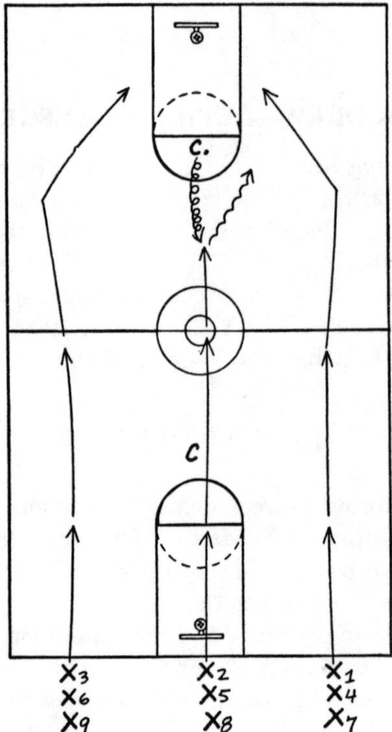

When X1, X2, X3 reach half-court, the second coach rolls a ball to X2 who picks the ball up and dribbles it to the free throw line. X1 and X3 stay wide and receive the pass from X2 for the power lay-up. If the shot is missed, the opposite man tips it in.

As soon as X1, X2, X3 sprint to half-court, the first coach brings X4, X5, X6 out. When X1, X2, X3 finish the fast break, they jog back to the end of the lines. The drill should run about four or five minutes.

COACH WAYNE M. MARTIN—MOREHEAD STATE UNIVERSITY

Coach Martin has been coaching for fifteen years. Ten of those fifteen have been at the college level. He has a won/lost record of 76 wins and 61 losses at Morehead State and 162 wins and 94 losses overall. His teams won three Kentucky Intercollegiate Athletic Conference championships and one NAIA District 23 championship. He was selected as Ohio Valley Conference Co-Coach of the Year in 1982.

FIGURE FOUR'S DRILL

Purpose: To improve defensive sliding techniques and conditioning
Personnel and Equipment Needed: Three managers or coaches, entire team of players and half-court
Teaching Points: 1) Keep shoulders square and head up. 2) Communicate when crossing paths. 3) Keep good, wide stance with tail down. 4) Slide on the balls of your feet.

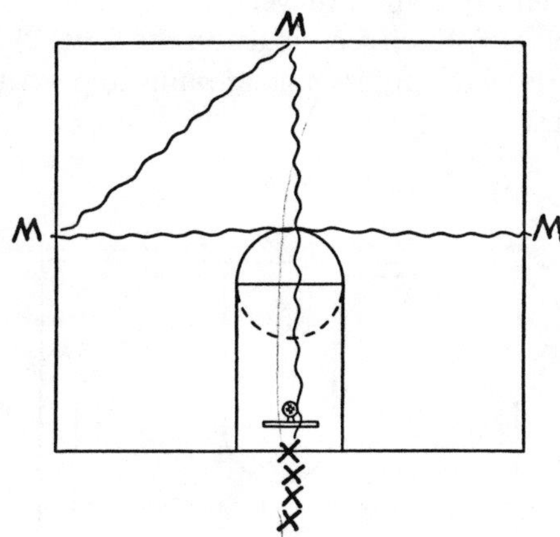

Directions: Have managers and/or coaches take the positions shown. Then have your entire team line up underneath the basket. The players advance from the baseline to the manager at mid-court with the close-out step. Once there, they slap the manager's hand and drop-step and lateral-slide to the next manager where they slap his hand and drop-step and lateral-slide to the last manager. At that point, they do five finger-tip push-ups and go to the end of the line. The next player in line goes as soon as the player in front of him crosses the free throw line. The second time through they reverse directions. They should go at least three times.

COACH TERRANCE J. O'CONNOR—FAIRFIELD UNIVERSITY

Coach O'Connor has been coaching for fourteen years. Eleven of those fourteen have been at the college level. He has an overall won/lost record of 89 wins and 82 losses. He was named Oswego County League Coach of the Year in 1972.

FIGURE EIGHT SPRINT AND SLIDE DRILL

Purpose: To improve a player's condition and defensive sliding ability

Personnel and Equipment Needed: A minimum of one player or a maximum of an entire team of players, and the entire floor

Teaching Points: 1) Keep feet apart on the slide. 2) Stay low and do not stand up on the slide. 3) Use a good jump stop when changing from a sprint to a slide.

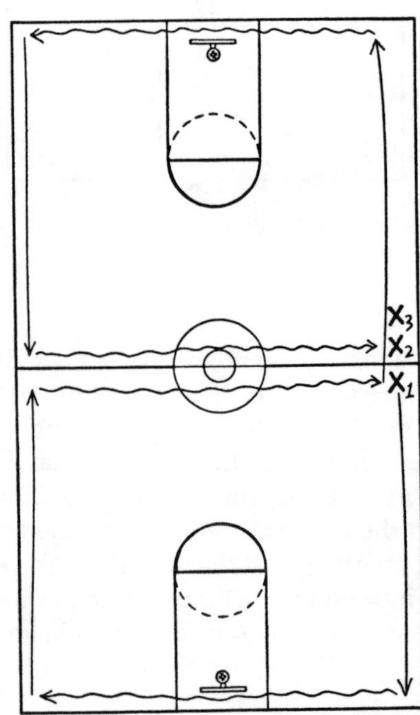

Directions: Have the players line up at half-court and face the baseline as shown. The first player in line O1 starts the drill by sprinting to the baseline. When he reaches the baseline he comes to a jump stop and begins a defensive slide along the baseline, facing the wall. When he reaches the corner he back-pedals to half-court where he makes a forward pivot and slides along the half-court line to the opposite sideline. When he reaches the opposite sideline he sprints to the baseline. At the baseline he makes a jump stop and slides to the other corner. When he reaches the corner he back-pedals to half-court. At half-court he makes a forward pivot and slides back to the starting point. Each player should do a minimum of three repetitions.

COACH RICH MARSHALL, ASSISTANT COACH—ARIZONA STATE UNIVERSITY

Coach Marshall has been coaching for four years. Three of those four years have been at the college level.

"DEVIL" DRILL

Purpose: To learn to take the charge and to block shots without fouling

Personnel and Equipment Needed: Entire team of players, two basketballs and the entire floor

Teaching Points: 1) Taking the charge: plant feet; hold position; arms up; do not shy away from contact. 2) Blocking shots: use arm closest to the baseline; time your jump.

Directions: Divide the entire squad into four lines, two facing each basket. The lines on end "A" should both start at the hash marks. On end "B" the defensive line should be at the free throw line extended and five feet in from the sideline, and the offensive line should be at the hash mark.

On end "A" the first offensive player (O) dribbles the ball hard to the basket for a lay-up. The defender (X) comes across and tries to block the shot with his inside hand (baseline side) without fouling the shooter. The ball is passed back to the offensive line and the drill continues. The first two players from end "A" go to end "B" to the ends of their respective lines (offense to offense and defense to defense). The next time they change ends they will change lines also.

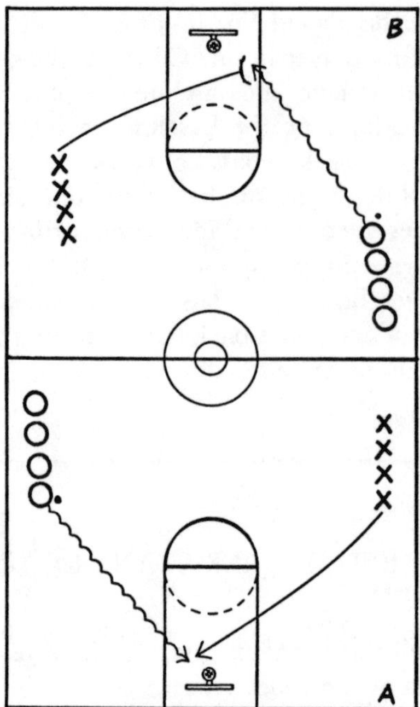

On end "B" the first offensive player (O) dribbles hard to the basket for a lay-up and the defender (X) should beat the offensive player to the box, square up and take the charge. The ball is passed back to the offensive line and the players go to end "A" to the ends of their respective lines (offense to offense and defense to defense). The next time they change ends they will change lines also. The drill continues until everyone has participated in each line.

COACH RICK HUCKABAY—MARSHALL UNIVERSITY

Coach Huckabay has been coaching for sixteen years. Four of those sixteen have been at the college level. He has an overall won/lost record of 310 wins and 51 losses. His high school teams won three state championships. He has been named High School Coach of the Year in Louisiana six times.

CHARGE AND POWER DRILL

Purpose: To learn to take the charge, then recover and power the ball to the basket

Personnel and Equipment Needed: Three managers, minimum of two players, two basketballs and a basket

Teaching Points: 1) Force the dribble to the middle. 2) Change directions and take the charge. 3) Recover and find the ball. 4) Power the ball to the basket with two people guarding you.

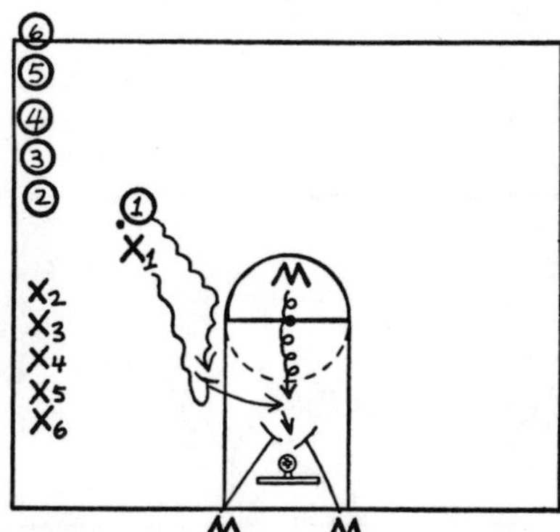

Directions: Divide the team into two groups, one offensive O's and one defensive X's along the sideline as diagrammed. X1 forces O1 to the free throw line; O1 changes directions and dribbles hard to the basket. X1 positions himself and takes the charge. As X1 draws the charge, manager 1 rolls another ball into the lane; at the same time managers 2 and 3 come on the floor as defensive players. X1 retrieves the second ball, powers it to the basket and tries to score against managers 2 and 3. The managers are instructed to foul and keep X1 from scoring. The drill ends when X1 scores. Then O2 and X2 come out and start the drill again.

COACH JEFF MEYER—LIBERTY BAPTIST COLLEGE

Coach Meyer has been coaching for seven years. Five of those seven have been at the college level. He has a won/lost record of 38 wins and 20 losses at Liberty Baptist. He was selected as NAIA District 19 Coach of the Year in 1982.

"TAKE THE CHARGE" DRILL

Purpose: To teach the technique of taking the charge on the baseline and diving on the floor for loose balls
Personnel and Equipment Needed: Two coaches or managers, minimum of two players, two basketballs and a basket
Teaching Points: 1) Deny the baseline drive. 2) Set up to take the charge. 3) Get up and find the loose ball and dive on the floor to gain possession.

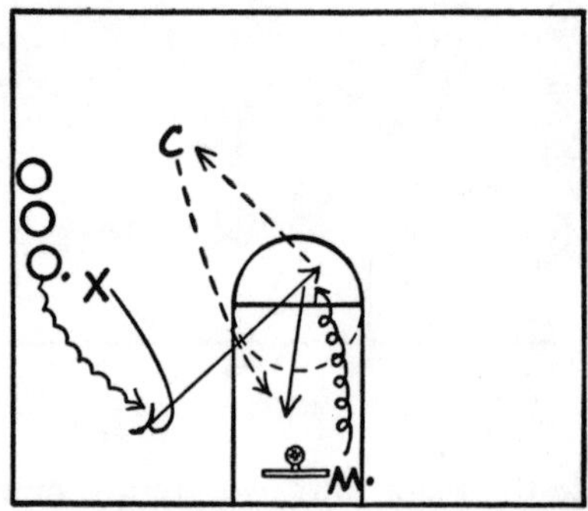

Directions: Line the team up at the free throw line extended. The first player in line comes out on defense and the next player has a ball and is offense. The offensive player drives baseline. The defensive player must beat him to the baseline and take the charge. On impact, the manager rolls a second ball into the lane. The defensive player who took the charge must immediately (after falling to the floor) look for the loose ball. He gets up and goes for the loose ball diving for it and pulling it into his body. While on the floor with the ball, the player must pass the ball to the coach and then get up and make a cut to the basket. The coach passes the ball back to him for a lay-up. The ball is given back to the manager. The offensive player becomes the new defensive player and the defensive player goes to the end of the line.

COACH LUTE OLSON—UNIVERSITY OF ARIZONA

Coach Olson has been coaching for twenty-six years. Ten of those twenty-six have been at the college level. He has an overall won/lost record of 191 wins and 93 losses. His teams shared the Big Ten Conference championship in 1979. His Iowa teams were the only Big Ten teams to make the NCAA every year from 1979 to 1982. He was named Big Ten Coach of the Year in 1979 and National Coach of the Year by *The Sporting News* and the National Association of Basketball Coaches in 1980.

LEAD PASS DENIAL DRILL

Purpose: To develop the skills necessary to deny the lead pass to the wing
Personnel and Equipment Needed: One passer, one offensive player, one defensive player, one basketball and one basket
Teaching Points: See Directions.

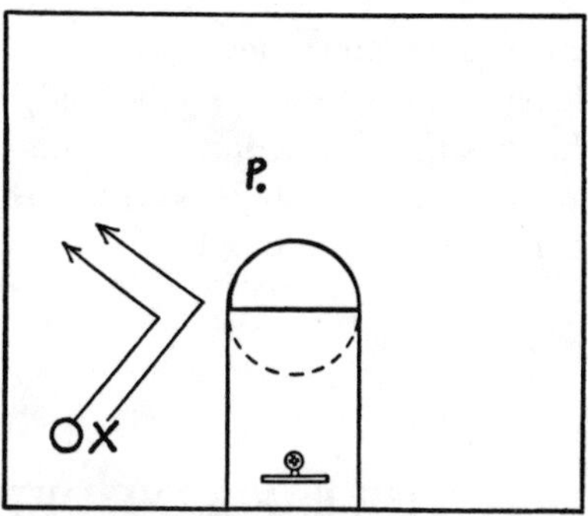

Directions: All the players line up along the baseline. The first two players step out onto the court, one on offense and one on defense. The passer, who is in a normal guard position, will slap the ball to start the drill. With the slap of the ball, the offensive player will make a V-type cut to try to get open in a normal forward position.

In attempting to deny the ball to the offensive player, the defender is to use the following teaching points:

1) The defender is to have the hand and arm nearest the passer fully extended into the passing lane. The palm of that hand is to be facing the passer (thumb down).
2) The arm nearest his opponent is to be placed in a flexed position with the arm bent at the elbow at a 90-degree angle. This position is called the "arm bar" position. The purpose of the arm bar is to keep the opponent from getting to the defender's feet, thereby limiting his foot movement.
3) The defender is to keep a gap between himself and his opponent until the offensive man reaches the free throw line extended. At that time, the defender is to make contact with his opponent with the arm bar. The reason for this is that the possibility of a backdoor cut becomes greater if there is no contact with the offensive player.
4) The defender is to keep his vision focused at the midpoint between the ball and the potential receiver. He should not look at the ball or at the offensive player.
5) The player is to stay in a low stance with a wide base. He is to avoid reaching or lunging for the ball. The defender must remember the importance of the head in maintaining balance.
6) The back leg is the power leg.
7) If the offensive player receives the ball, the defender is to readjust his position immediately so that his outside foot is pointing to the offensive player's crotch, thereby overplaying a "half-man" toward the baseline.

CUTTING OFF THE BASELINE DRIVE AND "BELLYING UP" DRILL

Purpose: To develop the skills necessary to successfully cut off any baseline drive attempt
Personnel and Equipment Needed: One passer, one offensive player, one defensive player, one basketball and one basket
Teaching Points: See Directions.

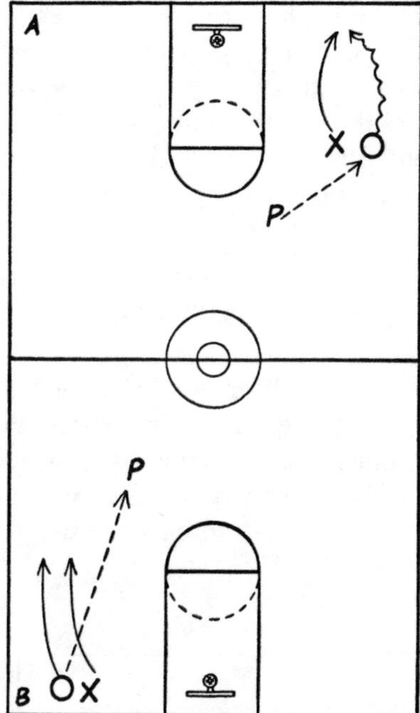

Directions: This drill is an extension of the lead pass denial drill. Once a pass is successfully made to the wing, the offensive player is to "face-up" immediately and attempt to drive the baseline. The defender takes an angle of retreat toward the baseline to cut the offensive player off. Once the offensive player has stopped his dribble, the defender makes a "dribble-kill" call indicating the dribble has been used and signaling all four teammates to get into the passing lanes and go for a five-second count. The offensive player is told to hold the ball for a two-count before throwing the ball back to the passer. This enables you to check the defender's foot position, belly-up position and "kill" call. Once the ball passes over the defender's hands, he is to jump immediately toward the ball and resume his denial position. (See Diagram B)

Teaching Points:

1) The defender is to cut the offensive player off by placing his baseline foot directly on the endline. His hands are to be up with his chest out to take any contact on the chest and avoid involving his hands, which might result in a reaching foul.

2) When the dribble has been picked up, the defender is to adjust his foot position so his back is "squared" to the high post area. This cuts off the potential pass to the area of the court that creates the largest number of problems for your defense.
3) The defender is to "mirror" the ball with his hands and try to get a deflection of the pass as it is made back out to the passer.

BACKDOOR COVERAGE DRILL

Purpose: To develop the skills to eliminate the backdoor cut
Personnel and Equipment Needed: One passer, one offensive player, one defensive player, one basketball and a basket
Teaching Points: 1) Stay in good defensive stance. 2) Make a quick head turn. 3) Get hand and arm into passing lane.

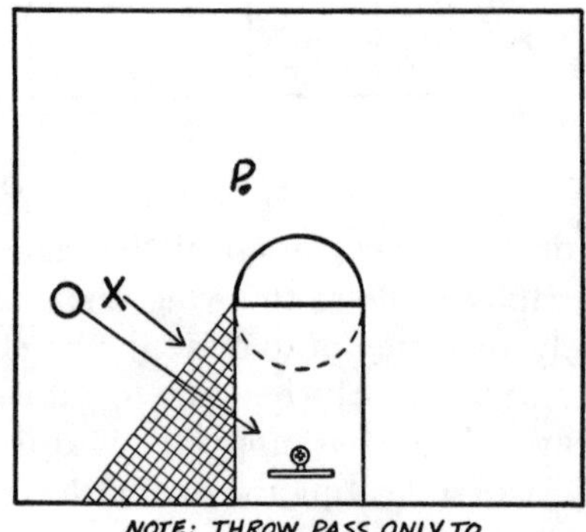

NOTE: THROW PASS ONLY TO SHADED AREA

Directions: This drill is another extension of the lead pass drill. The offensive player follows normal procedure for creating a lead pass. Once the offensive player has reached the free throw line extended, the passer fakes a pass, keying the backdoor cut by the offensive player. The defender is to retreat with the offensive player until vision is lost, at which time the defender is to snap his head over the shoulder closest to the basket in an effort to pick up vision on the ball. The hand and arm positions are switched quickly with the head turn. The hand and arm nearest the basket are thrown into the passing lane while the other hand

and arm will be placed in the arm bar position. If the offensive player does not receive the pass, he is to break out to lead position, with the defender reacting quickly to a lead pass defense position.

DEFENDING THE POST DRILL

Purpose: To improve the fundamentals of low post coverage
Personnel and Equipment Needed: Two passers, one offensive player, one defensive player, one basketball and a basket
Teaching Points: See Directions.

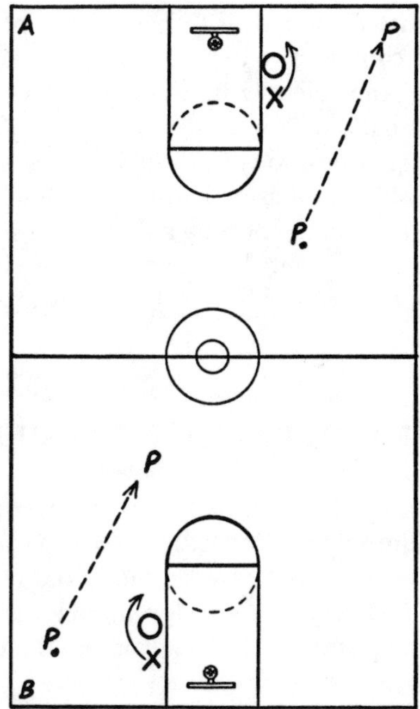

Directions: In this drill two passers are used with an offensive and defensive low post man. One passer is in the normal forward position, with the other one at the guard position. The defender is to protect the low post area as the ball is passed from the guard to the forward and the forward to the guard. The defender is to use the following low post rules or teaching points:

1) If the ball is above the free throw line extended, the defender is to be on the high side of the post in a three-quarter front position, with his denial hand and arm in the passing lane. His other hand and arm are in the arm bar position. The arm bar is to be used to keep the offensive post man from getting to the defender's legs and body.
2) If the ball is below the free throw line extended, the defender is to be on the low side of the post in a three-quarter front position. The normal lead hand and arm bar positions are used. (See Diagram B)
3) The exception to the above positions is if the post is below the "block" position. The defensive post should then be on the high side, regardless of the ball position. The reason for this is that if the ball is thrown to the post in that position, you can contain him behind the backboard and force him to "charge" the defender if he goes to the basket or be forced to pass the ball back out.
4) In changing positions from high to low side and vice versa, you should use a basic "half-moon" slide. This slide involves moving around the post by a direct face-to-face movement to the other position. The arm bar and lead hand position changes as one goes from high to low and vice versa.

DENYING THE LATERAL CUT (FLASH POST) DRILL

Purpose: To develop the skills necessary to cover the lateral cut
Personnel and Equipment Needed: Two passers, one offensive player, one defensive player, one basketball and a basket
Teaching Points: 1) Try to force (or funnel) the cutter above the third free throw lane position. 2) Do not allow the cutter to cut back-door.
Directions: Two passers are used in this drill, with one at the right guard position and the other at the left forward position. The drill starts with the ball in the offensive right forward position with the defender on him. He passes the ball to the guard position. The guard then throws the ball cross-court to the passer at the left forward position. The offensive player, after passing the ball to the guard, moves toward the baseline and as the ball is received by the forward he will try to "flash" to the ball. The defender "jumps" to the ball with each pass. As the offensive player breaks through the lane, the defender is to make contact with him

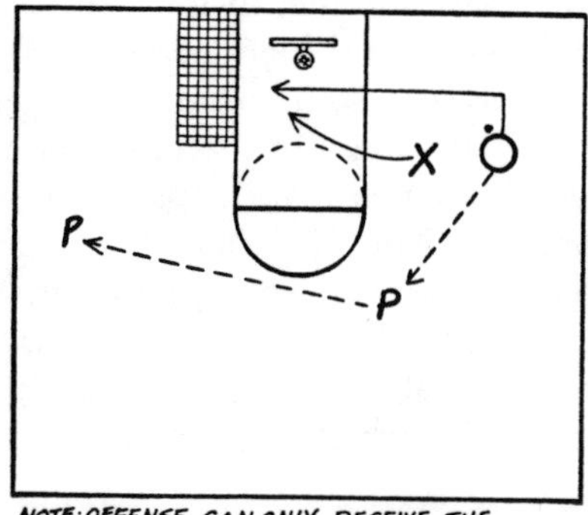

NOTE: OFFENSE CAN ONLY RECEIVE THE BALL IN THE SHADED RECTANGULAR AREA

as he reaches the middle of the lane. This contact is made with the arm bar, again trying to keep the offensive player from getting to his feet or body. *Note:* The offense can only receive the ball in the shaded rectangular area.

DEFENDING THE DIAGONAL CUT DRILL

Purpose: To improve the fundamentals necessary to eliminate the diagonal cut

Personnel and Equipment Needed: Two passers, one offensive player, one defensive player, one basketball and a basket

Teaching Points: 1) Establish contact with the offensive player as he makes contact with the lane during his cut. This body contact should be made with the arm bar. 2) "Funnel" the man away from the high post area. Force him outside of the circle by "riding" him up the lane.

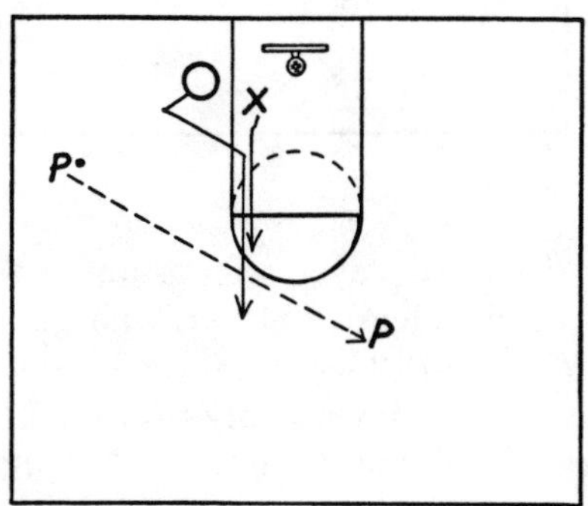

Directions: Two passers are used in this drill, with one at the right guard position and the other at the left forward position. The drill starts with the ball at the forward position and the offensive player in the block position on the ball side. On the pass from the forward to the guard, the offensive player takes two steps out toward the corner and then cuts hard toward the ball. The offensive player will attempt to get the ball in the high post area. The defender must make contact with him as he makes contact with the lane. He then funnels the man away from the high post area. Being able to defend against this cut is critical to stopping the backdoor play which is often used against a pressure-type defense.

ONE-ON-ONE OPERATIONAL DRILL

Purpose: To improve the techniques involved in on-the-ball defense
Personnel and Equipment Needed: Entire team, one basketball for every two players, one basket for every two players if possible, if not for every four players
Teaching Points: 1) Stress good on-the-ball defense. 2) On a shot attempt, the defender must try to: block the shot, change the shot, change the rhythm of the shooter or affect the shooter's vision.

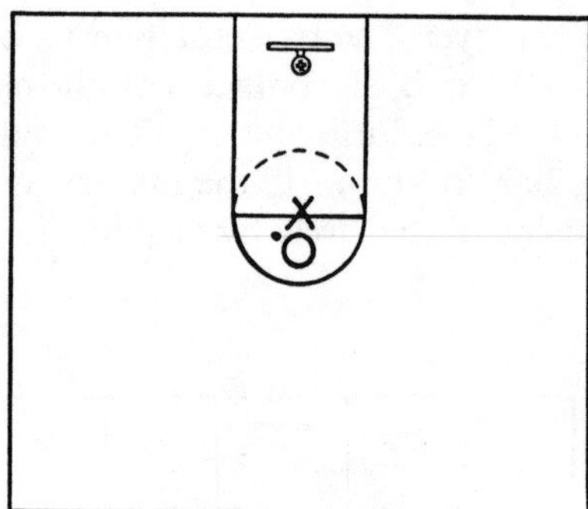

Directions: The defensive player, after assuming the defensive stance, will hand the ball to the offensive player, who has assumed a "ready" stance anywhere from 15 to 18 feet from the basket. Once the offensive player has received the ball, he has only two seconds in which to make his move. Once the offensive player takes the shot, the defensive player is required to pressure the shot. Once he has pressured the shot, he must yell "shot" to try to break the shooter's concentration, screen out and then rebound the ball if missed.

If the shot is made, the defensive player will take the ball and walk back to another position 15 to 18 feet from the basket and repeat the procedure. If the shot did not go in and the offensive player got the rebound inside the lane, he is to make a quick power move to the basket. If he rebounded it outside the lane, he is to hand the ball to the defensive player and take a position 15 to 18 feet from the basket for another attempt. If the defender rebounds the ball, he hands it to the offensive player and walks out 15 to 18 feet from the basket and assumes the offensive position. The games are played to seven or ten baskets.

Variations:

1) Allow the offensive player only one dribble.
2) Allow the offensive player two dribbles.
3) Allow the offensive player three dribbles, but require that one of those three must be a change-of-direction dribble.
4) Allow only jump shots.
5) Credit the offensive player with a basket for all offensive rebounds.
6) Allow either man who rebounds the ball to power the ball to the basket.

SEVEN-IN-ONE DRILL

Purpose: To develop individual on-the-ball and off-the-ball defensive skills

Personnel and Equipment Needed: Three passers, one offensive player, one defensive player, one basketball and a basket

Teaching Points: Emphasize those listed in the seven individual drills listed previously (lead pass denial, cutting off the baseline drive and "bellying up," backdoor coverage, defending the post, defending the diagonal cut and one-on-one operational).

Directions: Start this drill in the same position as described in the lead pass denial drill. The only difference is that you will add two passers to the one already described. This will give you one passer, for example, at the right guard position, one passer who is off the court near the right forward position, and a third passer at the left forward position.

The offensive player breaks out to receive the ball and continues to move until he receives the ball at the forward position. On reception of

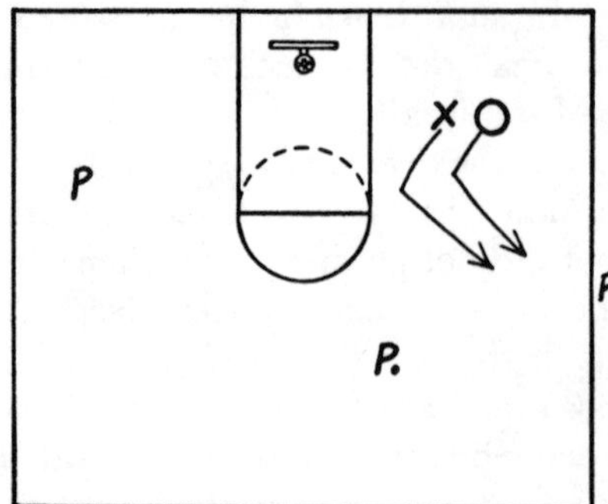

the ball he "faces-up" and immediately drives the baseline trying to "turn the corner." The defender must retreat and cut the man off as previously taught.

Once the man cuts the driver off, he follows the basic fundamentals taught in the belly-up and "kill" portion of the baseline drill. After two seconds, the offensive player passes the ball out to the original passer and tries to create another lead pass. If he is open, the passer gets him the ball and the offensive player again drives the baseline. He will continue to do this until he is denied the ball.

Once the man has been denied the ball, the passer gives a "ball fake" which keys the backdoor. The passer then tries to hit the cutter with a pass. The pass cannot be thrown into the lane because that coverage is the offside defender's responsibility.

The backdoor cut continues into the lane and if he has not received the ball, he cuts back to the ball side and takes a low post position above the block. At this point, the passer at the right forward position steps onto the court. The first passer at the guard position tries to feed the post. If the defender is denying the ball, it is then passed to the right forward passer who tries to get the ball to the post. The ball is then passed back and forth from the forward to guard positions, while the defender works on his "half-moon" slides.

Once the first passer decides the post coverage is acceptable, he will cross-court the ball to the left forward position. With that pass, the post man flashes across the lane trying to get the ball. The defender follows his flash post fundamentals in denying the ball. The cutter is restricted to receiving the ball from the third free throw position along the lane down to the baseline.

If the defender has denied the ball to the cutter, the forward passer will return the ball to the original passer position. With that pass, the cutter will attempt to make a diagonal cut into the top half of the free throw circle to receive the ball. The defender denies the ball as described in the "diagonal cut drill."

If the cutter is forced out of the circle, the passer gives the ball to the offensive player at the top of the key. At that time, the two go one-on-one under the regulations described in "one-on-one operational." The drill is complete once the shot has been taken and made or the miss rebounded by the defender.

You should use this drill, once the seven previously listed drills have been taught, as a review of the basic fundamentals. This drill has proved to be a great timesaving device.

COACH RICH MECKFESSEL—UNIVERSITY OF MISSOURI—ST. LOUIS

Coach Meckfessel has been coaching at the college level for fifteen years. He has a won/lost record of 265 wins and 181 losses. His teams won the West Virginia Intercollegiate Athletic Conference championship three times and the NAIA District 28 championship three times. They finished fourth at the NAIA tournament in 1967. He was named WVIAC Coach of the Year twice and NAIA Area VII Coach of the Year once.

SEVEN-POINT FORWARD DENIAL DRILL

Purpose: To teach forwards to deny a pass to their men

Personnel and Equipment Needed: Two coaches or managers, a minimum of four players, one basketball and one basket

Teaching Points: 1) Proper defensive stance. 2) Correct defensive positioning. 3) Extra effort to keep their men from catching the ball. 4) Do not allow the lob pass.

Directions: The manager or coach has the ball on the right side of the floor. The offensive man breaks out to catch the ball on the wing. The defensive man tries to deny him the ball, and if the ball can be passed to the offensive man, he passes it right back out. After about five seconds of this, the offensive man goes back door and the defense defends against it. Now the offensive man posts up low and the defensive man fronts him. After about five seconds, the coach yells "weak side" and the defensive man breaks into the lane; then the offensive man tries to flash to the ball

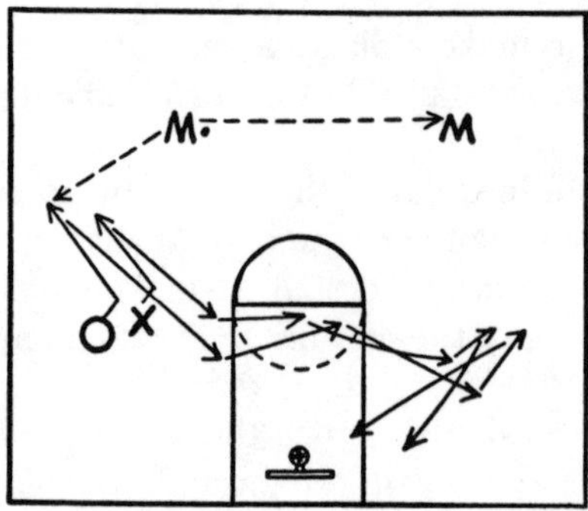

which has been passed to the second manager or coach on the other side. From there, the offensive man tries to catch the ball on the wing, then back door and finally low post on the other side. The seven points are: 1) wing denial on the right side; 2) back door on the right side; 3) low post on the right side; 4) flash post from right side to left side; 5) wing denial on left side; 6) back door on the left side; and 7) low post on the left side. Upon completion of the drill, the first two players rest and two more do the drill. Then the first two players come back out and reverse roles (offense becomes defense). The defense is allowed to give up no more than seven catches over the seven-point sequence.

COACH BILL MORSE—FORT HAYS STATE UNIVERSITY

Coach Morse has been coaching for twenty-one years. Thirteen of those twenty-one have been at the college level. He compiled a won/lost record of 32 wins and 4 losses in his first year at Fort Hays State and has 228 wins and 70 losses overall at the college level. His teams won the Great Lakes Conference in 1980 and the Central States Intercollegiate Conference in 1983. His 1980 team finished fourth in the NAIA tournament and his 1983 team finished third. He was selected NAIA District 23 Coach of the Year in 1978 and 1980. He was also selected Kansas Basketball Coaches Association Coach of the Year and NAIA Area 4 Coach of the Year in 1983.

CALIFORNIA DRILL

Purpose: To teach defensive positioning and how to defense the baseline cut

Personnel and Equipment Needed: Minimum of six players, one coach, one basketball and a basket

Teaching Points: 1) See the man and the ball at all times. 2) Do not allow your man to get behind you. 3) Communicate. 4) Beat the offense to the spot.

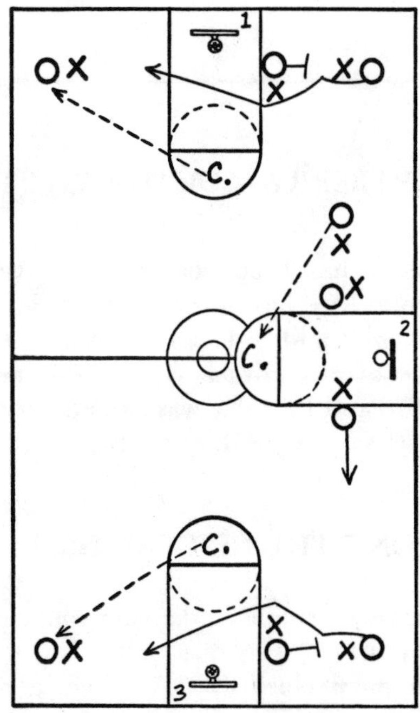

Directions: Position two offensive players in each corner with defenders and one offensive player with defender on one of the blocks. A coach lines up with a ball at the top of the circle. On the coach's pass to the corner away from the picker, we get a baseline cut. On the return pass to the coach and a pass to the other corner we get another baseline cut and continuity. The ball side defender must apply intelligent pressure on the ball. The defender guarding the picker must loosen up and see both man and ball. The man guarding the cutter must sprint to the lane on the guard-to-forward pass. He must not allow himself to get picked. He gets on the ball side of the pick seeing both the ball and his man flashing to the ball. He does not allow his man to get behind him. Always stay belly-up to your man. After the defense has gone through this several times, have the offense and defense change positions.

Variations:

1) Have the picker post up or pick away.
2) Have the baseline cutter come to high post off the pick and then slide to the basket.

COACH BOB DERRYBERRY—SOUTHWEST TEXAS STATE UNIVERSITY

Coach Derryberry has been coaching for twenty-three years. Twelve of those twenty-three have been at the college level. He has a won/lost record of 34 wins and 20 losses at Southwest Texas State and 471 wins and 191 losses overall. His teams won the Lone Star Conference title in 1976, 1977, 1978 and 1981. He was named Lone Star Conference Coach of the Year in 1976 and 1981.

FRONT THE CUTTER DRILL

Purpose: To improve your skills in denying your man the ball when he is cutting to the basket

Personnel and Equipment Needed: A coach, a minimum of two players, one basketball and a basket

Teaching Points: 1) On the pass, move in direction of the pass. 2) Keep your arm in the passing lane. 3) Maintain vision with your man and the ball at all times.

Directions: The defensive player (X) has the ball. He lines himself up on the offensive player. Example: He splits the offensive player down the middle and also lines his feet up in a toe-heel alignment, influencing the offensive player to the nearest sideline. When he is ready, the defensive player gives the ball to the offensive player (O). The offensive player passes the ball to the coach. On the pass, the defensive player jumps in

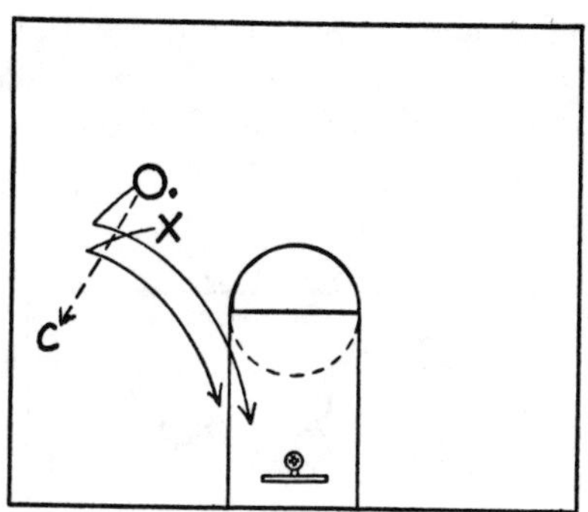

the direction of the pass, maintaining vision with the ball and his man. The offensive player makes a "V" cut to the basket. The defensive player follows the offense with his back to the ball, yet at all times staying between his man and the ball and keeping vision with both his man and the ball. Once the offensive player gets to the block, he pauses for a second. Then he breaks to the sideline and back to the basket. The defensive player again has his back to the ball, staying between his man and the ball, maintaining vision with his man and the ball and keeping his lead arm and hand out in the passing lane.

Note: In order for the defensive player to maintain vision, he will at times have to rotate his head from shoulder to shoulder. During the split second that he turns his head he will lose eye contact with the ball.

COACH JIM DAFLER—MOUNT UNION COLLEGE

Coach Dafler has been coaching for ten years all at the college level. He has a seven-year won/lost record of 86 wins and 70 losses. His teams won the Presidents' Athletic Conference championship in 1978 and 1982. He was selected as Presidents' Athletic Conference Coach of the Year in 1978 and 1982.

HALF-COURT TRANSITION DRILL

Purpose: To improve the transition from offense to defense
Personnel and Equipment Needed: A minimum of six players, one basketball and a basket

Teaching Points: 1) Force the ball into the weak hand. 2) Make the offense pick up their dribble. 3) Convert quickly from offense to deny the inbounds pass. 4) Total denial to get the five-second count.

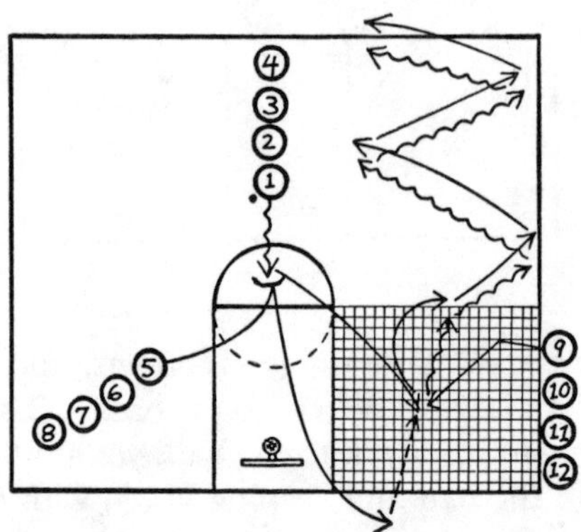

Directions: Have your players divide equally into three lines; one at the center circle, one in the right hand corner and one on the left sideline.

The drill starts with O1 coming on the dribble to score against O5. O5 plays proper one-on-one transition defense and O1 attempts to go all the way to the basket for the score under control. When O5 gains possession of the ball from a rebound, steal or score, he takes the ball out quickly for a throw-in to O9. After losing possession, O1 converts quickly to defense to deny the inbounds pass to O9. O9 must receive the pass in the shaded area to prevent the long pass and to make O9 work on his moves to get open. Once O9 gets the ball, he dribbles up the court with O1 playing defense on him. At the half-court line, O9 hands the ball to O2 who attacks O6 to start a new cycle. The players rotate as follows: O9 gets in line behind O4, O1 rotates to the line behind O8, and O5 gets in line behind O12. The drill continues until everyone has played each position.

COACH GEORGE BLANEY—HOLY CROSS COLLEGE

Coach Blaney has been coaching for eighteen years. Sixteen of those eighteen have been at the college level. He has a won/lost record of

191 wins and 124 losses overall. His teams won the ECAC tournament championship in 1977 and 1980. He was selected New England Coach of the Year in 1975 and Eastern Coach of the Year in 1977.

ONE-ON-ONE MIDCOURT DRILL

Purpose: To improve defensive sliding and one-on-one play
Personnel and Equipment Needed: A minimum of two players, one basketball and a basket
Teaching Points: 1) Position defensively on ball side. 2) Remain in good defensive stance. 3) Keep hands active on defense. 4) Block out after the shot.

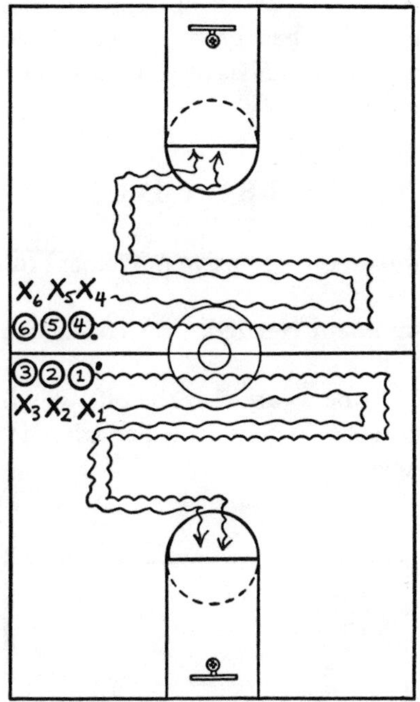

Directions: Have the players line up in two lines on the sideline at midcourt, one offensive line O1 and one defensive line X1. To start the drill, O1 dribbles the ball across the court. X1 slides in a defensive stance with his hands active and constantly in a down low position. The defense must stay on the ball and, therefore, generally ahead of the offensive man. O1 dribbles across the court and then back to the starting point, and then to the middle of the floor. From this point, they play one-on-one to the basket. Defensively, we are attempting to turn the dribbler, to make the offense pull up for the jumper, or to take an offensive charge. After the shot, a block out must be made. Do this with all the players, with each player getting to play defense at least three times.

COACH ED GREEN—ROANOKE COLLEGE

Coach Green has been coaching for twenty years. Nine of those twenty have been at the college level. He has a won/lost record of 146 wins and 26 losses at Roanoke for an outstanding .849 winning percentage. His teams have won the Old Dominion Athletic Conference championship three times. He has been named National Association of Basketball Coaches, NCAA Division III, District Coach of the Year three of the last four years.

TWO-BALL DRILL

Purpose: To improve the defensive movement of the weak side players

Personnel and Equipment Needed: A coach, four players, two basketballs and a basket

Teaching Points: 1) Be aware that the offense will try to get the ball to the weak side to score. 2) Stay in a flat triangle to maintain visual contact with your own man.

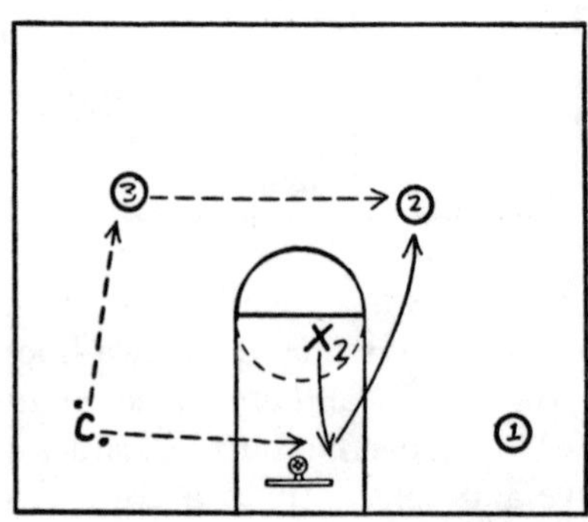

Directions: The coach is in the corner with two basketballs. He begins the drill by passing the first ball to O1. The defensive player X2 must drop back and deflect that pass. As soon as he has passed the first ball, the coach passes the second ball around to O3 and then to O2 or directly to O2 by using a skip pass. X2 must recover to O2 who is the shooter and play defense. Have the defensive player go twice and then rotate clockwise. O1 becomes X2, O2 becomes O1, O3 becomes O2, and X2 becomes O3.

COACH CHARLIE BOWEN—PENN STATE UNIVERSITY—CAPITOL CAMPUS

Coach Bowen has been coaching for ten years. Two of those ten have been at the college level. At Susquehanna Community High School in 1978 his team played for the district championship, the first time in the school's history. At Dallastown Area High School his won/lost record was 29 wins and 22 losses. In 1982, he was the runner-up to the York County Interscholastic Athletic Association Coach of the Year, and in 1977 he was selected as the coach of the "Dream Game" all-star game.

ZONE PRESS REACTION DRILL

Purpose: To improve defensive reaction time from different positions. To determine which player should be your stealer in your zone press
Personnel and Equipment Needed: Minimum of five players, one coach, one basketball, and half of the court
Teaching Points: 1) Do not turn your head on the ball. 2) Keep your feet moving. 3) React on the pass.
Directions: The coach is positioned at the center circle with a defensive man in front of him. Four other players are positioned on the floor (as shown), two at the wings and two in the corners. The defensive man has the ball and he starts the drill by handing the ball to the coach. He then hustles back to the free throw line in a defensive stance. The coach passes to any of the four offensive players and the defensive man must react to the pass. If he intercepts the pass, he passes it back to the coach and the players rotate positions with a new defensive man coming out. If he does not intercept the pass, the offensive player passes it back to the

coach and the defensive man hustles back to the free throw line to try again. The defense must keep going until the coach chooses another one. The drill continues until everyone has been on defense.

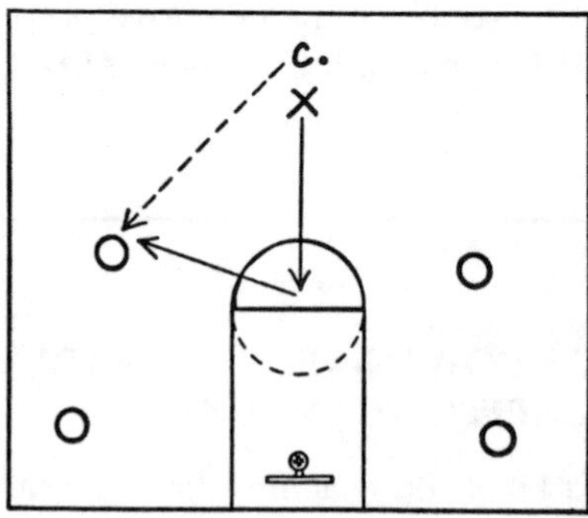

COACH RICH GRAWER—ST. LOUIS UNIVERSITY

Coach Grawer has been coaching for seventeen years. Two of those seventeen have been at the college level. He has an overall won/lost record of 316 wins and 125 losses. His teams at Desmet High School won the Missouri Large School state championship in 1972–73, 1977–78 and 1978–79.

SHOT BLOCKER DRILL

Purpose: To develop quick hand and leg reaction
Personnel and Equipment Needed: A minimum of five players, one basketball and a basket
Teaching Points: 1) React quickly to the ball. 2) Try to distract the shooter or block his shot.
Directions: Have the players align themselves as shown. O4 has the ball. X5 is a post player in defensive position facing the offensive players O1, O2 and O3. The drill begins with O4 passing the ball to one of the three offensive players. X5 must react to the pass and try to distract the shooter or block his shot. The offensive players are instructed, upon receiving the pass, to power the ball toward the basket. Contact results, but it is fun.

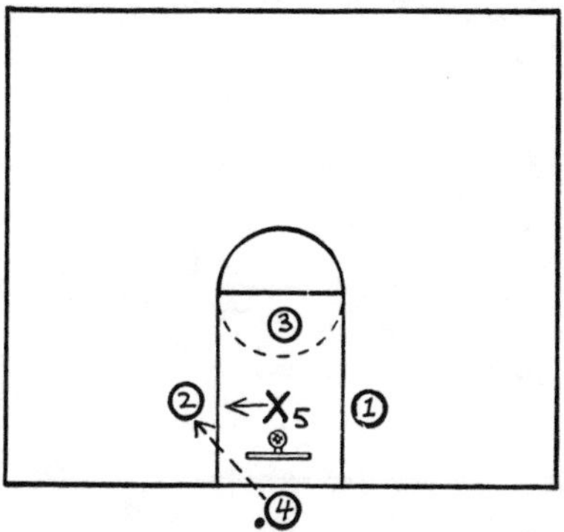

COACH BILL KALBAUGH—MERCYHURST COLLEGE

Coach Kalbaugh has been coaching for thirteen years. Eleven of those thirteen have been at the college level as either an assistant or a head coach. While an assistant at St. Bonaventure University for seven years, his teams had a won/lost record of 115 wins and 60 losses. They had two post-season appearances in the NIT and won that tournament in 1977 and one post-season appearance in the NCAA. Since his coming to Mercyhurst College, the basketball program has shown improvement each year. They finished the 1983–84 season with a won/lost record of 15 wins and 12 losses which is the best record at Mercyhurst in the past six years.

POPCORN DRILL

Purpose: To improve the techniques of wing denial and recovering to the shooter

Personnel and Equipment Needed: Two coaches, a minimum of three players, two basketballs and a basket

Teaching Points: 1) Keep arm up and leg out to deny pass. 2) Open up when your man goes back door. 3) React to shooter to bother him on his shot. 4) Block out shooter after the shot.

Directions: One line of offensive players (O2) lines up in the corner; they are the shooters. Another line of offensive players (O1) lines up at the free throw line extended. And a third line of players (X1) defends against O1. The two coaches have the basketballs and stand in position to pass to the wing and to the corner. The drill begins with O1 trying to

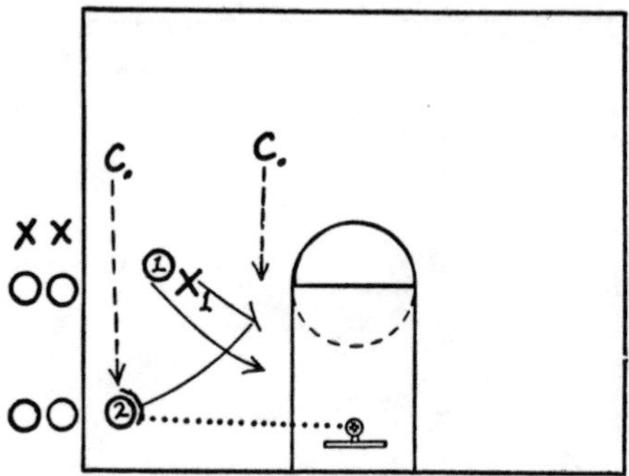

beat X1 back door. On the back door cut, the first coach passes the ball to O1 and X1 opens up and knocks the ball away. As soon as this happens, the second coach passes his ball to O2 the shooter in the corner. The defensive player X1 must react to the corner and try to bother the shooter on his jump shot. After the shot, he blocks out the shooter to finish the drill. Then the next player in each line comes out and the drill is repeated. Those coming off go to different lines until they have participated in each of the three spots.

COACH MAX GOOD—EASTERN KENTUCKY UNIVERSITY

Coach Good has been coaching for fourteen years. Eight of those fourteen have been at the college level as either an assistant or a head coach. Before his coming to Eastern Kentucky, his teams posted a won/lost record of 53 wins and 27 losses in the three years he was the head coach. He was selected as Central Kentucky Conference Coach of the Year in 1974–75 when his team had a 24–5 record.

ANTICIPATION DRILL

Purpose: To improve the anticipation of defensive players to help out on the open man

Personnel and Equipment Needed: A minimum of six players, two coaches, one basketball and a basket

Teaching Points: 1) Force the offense to pick-up their dribble. 2) React on the passes. 3) Help out on the open man. 4) Position to take the charge.

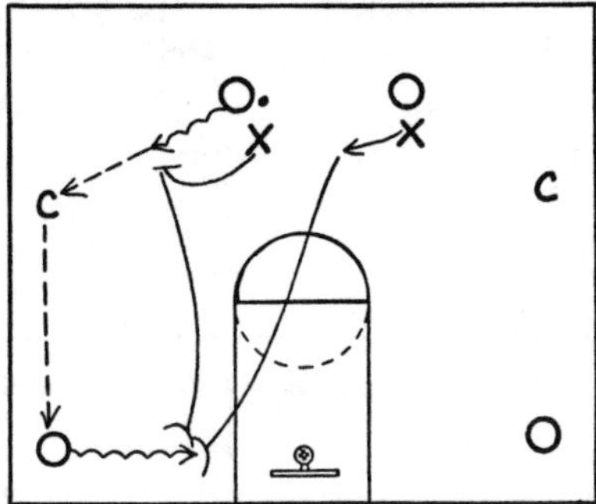

Directions: The two coaches position themselves at the hash marks. The two unguarded players are placed in the corners and the remaining four players go two-on-two against each other. Start the drill with the two offensive players going live against the two defensive players. If the defense makes the offense pick up its dribble, the offense must pass to one of the coaches. When the pass goes to the coaches, the defense adjusts their positions accordingly (denial and help). If the coach passes the ball to the corner to the unguarded player, he takes it on the dribble up the baseline to the basket. Both defenders drop to the baseline to take the charge and stop the ball. The players rotate as follows: The offense goes to defense, the defense goes to the unguarded offense and the unguarded offense goes to offense. The drill continues until all the players have played each of the three positions.

COACH JOHN WEINERT—BOWLING GREEN UNIVERSITY

Coach Weinert has been coaching for twenty-one years. Seventeen of those twenty-one have been at the college level. He has a won/lost record of 109 wins and 88 losses at Bowling Green and 322 wins and 201 losses overall. His teams won the Mid-American Conference championships in 1980, 1981and 1983. He has been named Coach of the Year five times in three different college conferences.

GET BACK DRILL

Purpose: To improve the following aspects of the game: passing, rebounding defense and conditioning

Personnel and Equipment Needed: One coach, a minimum of eight players, one basketball and the entire floor
Teaching Points: 1) Make a good overhead outlet pass. 2) Hustle back on defense and play aggressive two-on-two.

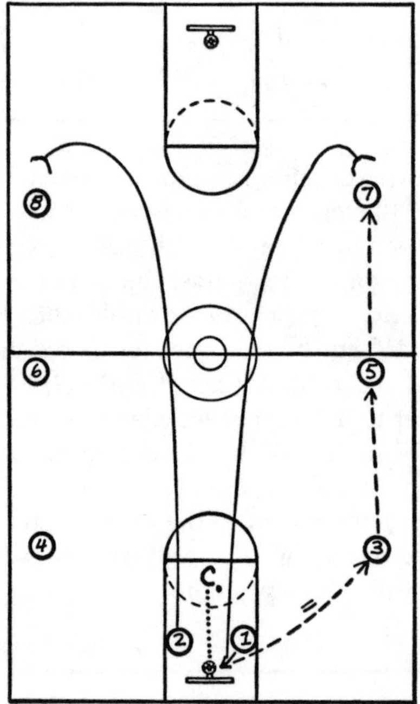

Directions: Position your players as shown above. The coach begins the drill by tossing the ball up on the board. O1 or O2 will rebound the ball, depending on which side of the board it comes off, and will outlet it to the outlet man on his side of the floor. In the diagram, O1 rebounds the ball and outlets it to O3. O3 passes it to O5 who passes it on to O7. O7 and O8 take the ball two-on-two against O1 and O2 who hustled down the floor to play defense after the ball was outletted. After the assault is over, the players rotate as follows: O3 and O4 replace O1 and O2, O5 and O6 replace O3 and O4; O7 and O8 replace O5 and O6, and O1 and O2 replace O7 and O8.

COACH JEFF SIMONS—JOHN BROWN UNIVERSITY

Coach Simons has been coaching for eighteen years. Fifteen of those eighteen have been at the college level. He has an overall won/lost record of 249 wins and 195 losses. His team won the National Junior College Athletic Association Region Six championship and he was named Region Six Coach of the Year.

SIX-MAN DRILL

Purpose: To improve defensive techniques for inside players
Personnel and Equipment Needed: A minimum of six players, one basketball and a basket
Teaching Points: 1) Defend ball side low, mid and high posts. 2) Defend help side. 3) Defend against screens, both on the ball side and the help side. 4) Defend weak side cuts to the ball. 5) Blocking off the boards.

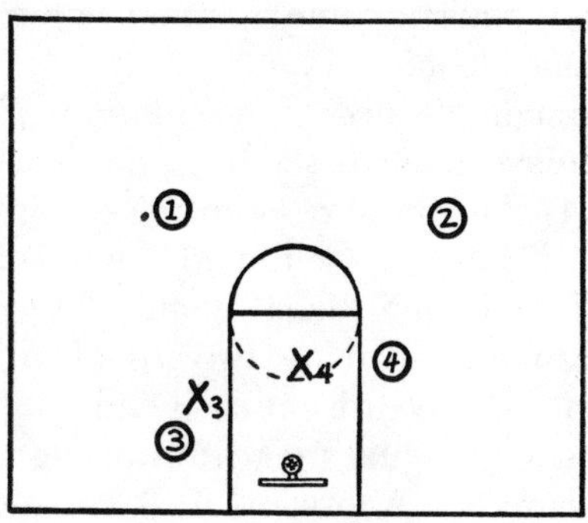

Directions: Players O1 and O2 are stationary offensive passers. O3 and O4 are the inside offensive players and X3 and X4 are their defenders. The drill begins with the ball at either O1 or O2. O3 and O4 play live two-on-two with X3 and X4, with the emphasis on the defense. The offensive players (O3 and O4) can screen for each other, cut to the ball, post up, crisscross and try to score on X3 and X4. However, they can only score inside the key. After one offensive thrust, everyone rotates one position clockwise.

COACH BOBBY HUSSEY—DAVIDSON COLLEGE

Coach Hussey has been coaching for eighteen years. Twelve of those eighteen have been at the college level. He has an overall won/lost record of 213 wins and 139 losses.

ONE-ON-ONE PLUS TWO DRILL

Purpose: To create a realistic game situation with combinations of all the individual defensive techniques

Personnel and Equipment Needed: A minimum of six players and a maximum of twelve players, one basketball and the entire court

Teaching Points: 1) Ball pressure—control the dribbler. 2) Defense on the ball—measure distance. 3) Communication. 4) Help and recover. 5) Screens on and off the ball. 6) Blocking out. 7) Offensive boards.

Directions: The team is divided into two groups with two guards, two forwards and two centers (forwards) at each end.

The drill begins with a guard (O1) advancing the ball down the court against the defense X1. A forward (O2) and a center (O3) move onto the court and try to get open. X2 and X3 take up proper defensive positions. As O1 crosses half-court, three-on-three play begins. Once a basket is scored, O4 advances the ball down the court against X4. O5 and O6 move onto the court and try to get open. X5 and X6 take up proper defensive positions. As O4 brings the ball across half-court, three-on-three play begins. After a basket, the drill continues.

Variation: This drill can also be run with two guards (O1 and O2) going against two defenders (X1 and X2). The forwards and centers are the same as before.

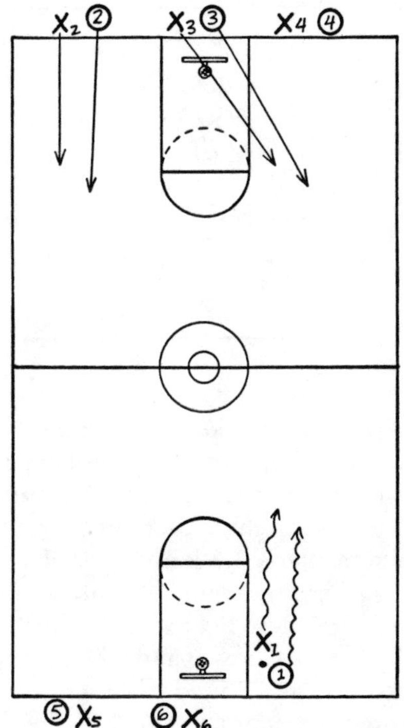

COACH RON BISHOP—TENNESSEE TEMPLE UNIVERSITY

Coach Bishop has been coaching for eight years all at the college level. He has compiled a won/lost record of 206 wins and 73 losses. His teams won the National Christian College Athletic Association national championship in 1979, 1981, 1982 and 1983. He was selected as NCCAA National Coach of the Year in 1979.

THREE-ON-THREE DEFENSIVE DRILL

Purpose: To teach players to play man-to-man defense without switching on picks

Personnel and Equipment Needed: Minimum of six players, one basketball and a basket

Teaching Points: 1) Jump in on picks. 2) Weak side help. 3) Fight over picks—never go behind the pick.

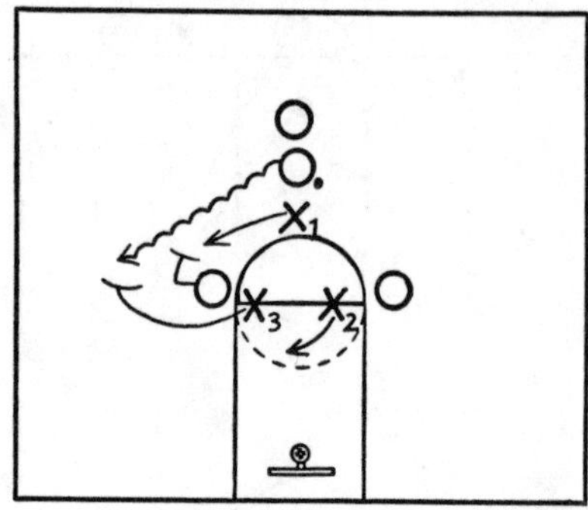

Directions: Have the players take their positions on the floor as diagrammed. As O1 dribbles to his right, X1 plays nose on the ball. O2 and O3 are at the free throw line in the corners and are stationary, setting picks for O1. As O1 dribbles right, X3 must call out the pick and jump in on O1, forcing him to charge, pick up his dribble, or swing wide. At the same time, X2 sags into the middle, giving weak side help to take away the roll by O3. X1 needs to fight over the top of the pick; he never goes behind. X3 will just show himself and then jump back to O3. There is no switching. The drill can be used to either side. After a couple of turns the players switch positions and continue the drill until everyone has played every position.

COACH DAN HAYS—NORTHWESTERN OKLAHOMA STATE UNIVERSITY

Coach Hays has been coaching for fifteen years. Nine of those fifteen have been at the college level. He has an overall won/lost record of 230 wins and 153 losses. His team won the Oklahoma Intercollegiate Conference championship in 1981. He was selected as NAIA District 9 Coach of the Year and Oklahoma Intercollegiate Conference Coach of the Year in 1981.

THREE-ON-THREE BREAKDOWN DRILL

Purpose: To teach players to cover down on baseline penetration
Personnel and Equipment Needed: The entire team, two basketballs and the full court

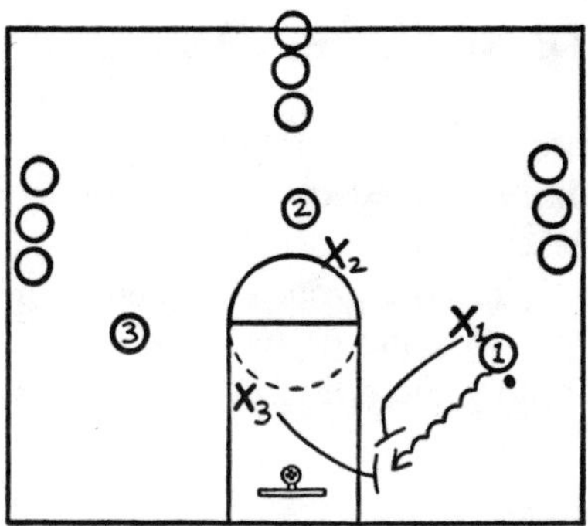

Teaching Points: 1) Sprint and close out to help on penetration.
Directions: Divide the team into three lines as shown. The first player in each line comes out to play defense on the next player in line who is on offense. O1 has the ball and starts with an advantage on X1 and dribbles the baseline to the basket to try to score. X1 sprints to try to cut off O1 and X3 must sprint to stop the penetration and trap with X1. X2 must cover down to the baseline to stop the pass across the lane. When O1 is stopped, he passes the ball out to O2, and X2 and X3 must close out on their men and then play live three-on-three. When the defense rebounds the made or missed shot, they fast-break to the opposite end and convert. The players rotate in the following manner: offense goes to defense, the next player in line becomes the offense and the defense goes to the end of the line. The drill continues until everyone has played defense.

COACH EDDIE SUTTON—UNIVERSITY OF ARKANSAS

Coach Sutton has been coaching for twenty-three years. Fourteen of those twenty-three have been at the college level. He has a won/lost record of 213 wins and 55 losses at Arkansas for a .795 winning percentage. His overall won/lost record is 296 wins and 105 losses. His teams have won the Southwest Conference championship five out of the last six years. They also won the NCAA Western Regional in 1978. He was named Southwest Conference Coach of the Year in 1975, 1977, 1979 and 1981. He was named National Coach of the Year in 1977 and 1978.

STATIONARY SHELL DEFENSE DRILL

Purpose: To improve defensive movement as a unit
Personnel and Equipment Needed: A minimum of eight players, one basketball and a basket
Teaching Points: 1) Keep a protective shell around the scoring area. 2) Know whether you are one or two passes away from the ball. 3) Achieve a ball-you-man philosophy.

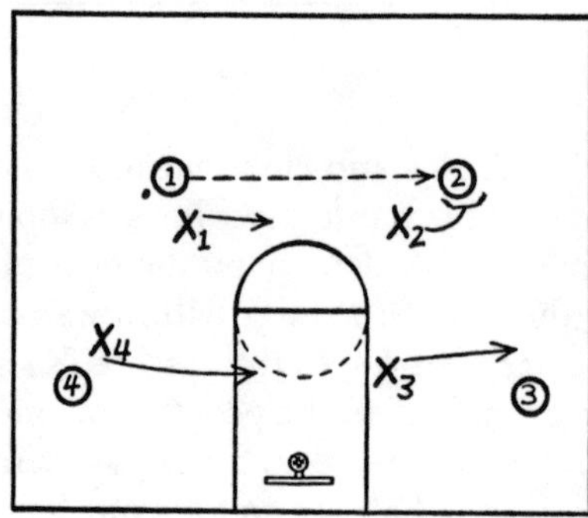

Directions: Have four offensive players assume their positions around the perimeter. Then the defensive players assume their positions in relation to their men and the ball. If the ball is two passes away, you should be one step off a line between your man and the ball (flat triangle) and opened up to the ball so that you can see your man and the ball. If the ball is only one pass away, you jump toward the ball in a good defensive stance.

The drill begins with the ball at O1. The ball is then passed around the perimeter, with the defense shifting while each pass is in the air. The defense allows the pass to the next man, but is allowed to intercept any skip pass. The drill should continue for a couple of minutes and then change the offense to defense and defense to offense.

COACH GARY SMITH—UNIVERSITY OF REDLANDS

Coach Smith has been coaching for eighteen years. Eleven of those eighteen have been at the college level. He has an overall won/lost record of 246 wins and 195 losses. His teams won the S.C.I.A.C. championship in 1976 and 1982. He was selected as NAIA District 3 and Area 1 Coach of the Year in 1976.

FOUR-ON-FOUR CONTINUOUS DEFENSE DRILL

Purpose: To work on the transition from offense to defense and on particular aspects of team defense
Personnel and Equipment Needed: A coach, a minimum of twelve players, a basketball and the entire floor
Teaching Points: 1) Sprint to defense. 2) See the ball as you sprint to defense. 3) Talk as you pick up your men—talk often and loud. 4) Flow immediately into pressure defense: close lanes, help, help the helper, etc.

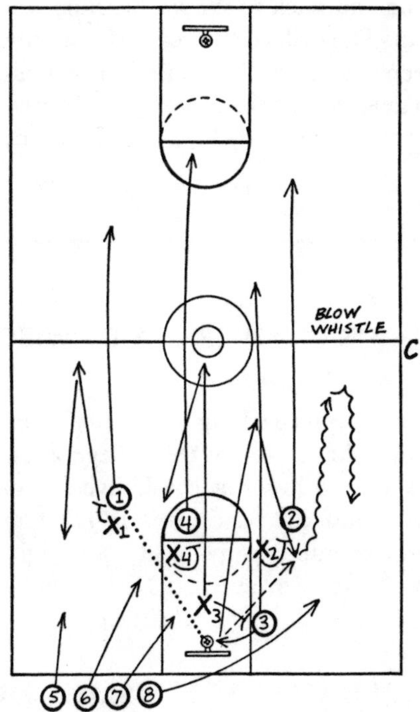

Directions: Divide your players into three teams of four each. Have two of the three teams go out on the floor, with one on offense and one on defense. The offensive team (O1, O2, O3 and O4) runs a half-court motion offense against the defense. They keep running the offense until they get a good shot or a turnover occurs. On a turnover or a defensive rebound, the team coming up with the ball goes on a break, while the team that was on offense sprints to defense at the other end. The new offensive team (X1, X2, X3 and X4) now runs the same motion offense that had just been run against them if they did not score on the break. This continues until the coach blows his whistle. The coach can blow his whistle at any time during this phase.

Blow it early, just after the offensive team has passed half-court in their transition, and sometimes later, after the offensive team has begun running the motion offense. When the whistle blows, the team that is on offense immediately turns around and attacks the basket at the opposite end. They do not wait for the new group to get set up. The third group (O5, O6, O7 and O8 which has been standing under the basket) steps quickly onto the floor and picks up their men and moves into its pressure defense. The team that was on defense when the whistle blew runs around the sideline and back to the far baseline where they await their next turn to step in. The drill continues in this manner with the constant continuity between offense and defense. On a made basket, the team scoring sprints to defense and the other team rips the ball out of the basket and goes with the ball quickly, not bothering to take it out of bounds.

COACH STAN JACK—UNIVERSITY OF WISCONSIN—RIVER FALLS

Coach Jack has been coaching for twenty-seven years. Twenty-two of those twenty-seven have been at the college level. He has a won/lost record of 38 wins and 15 losses at the University of Wisconsin—River Falls, and 437 wins and 209 losses overall. His teams have won seven college conference championships and two high school conference championships. He has been selected NAIA District 15 Coach of the Year and NAIA District7 Coach of the Year.

CUTTHROAT SCRIMMAGE DRILL

Purpose: To quicken your defensive pick-up coverage
Personnel and Equipment Needed: Two coaches or managers, a minimum of 15 players, three sets of colored jerseys, one basketball and a basket

Teaching Points: 1) Quickly pick up players defensively. 2) Make good outlet pass after gaining the defensive rebound.

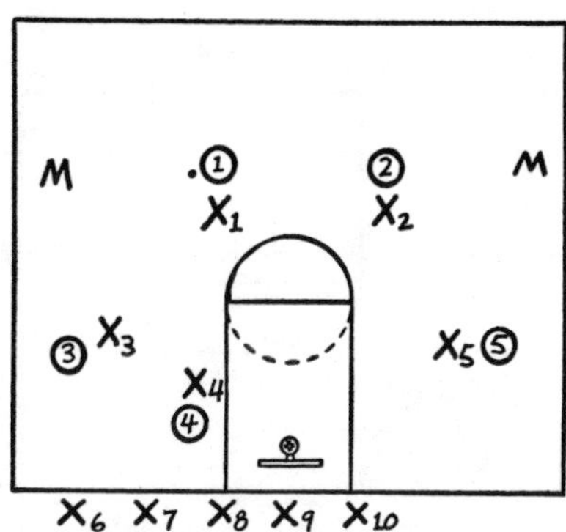

Directions: As shown, O1-O5 are on offense working their set offense. X1-X5 are on defense and will make an outlet pass to the managers after gaining the defensive rebound.

The offensive team will stay on offense as long as they score. The defensive team will remain on defense as long as they are scored upon.

X6-X10 are along the baseline ready to come in on defense when there is a defensive rebound and an outlet pass to the managers. The defensive rebounding team converts to offense quickly and the offensive team that failed to score goes out to the side, then to the baseline. Have the managers yell "outlet, outlet" on the rebound.

COACH KEN STIBLER—BISCAYNE COLLEGE

Coach Stibler has been coaching for twenty-four years at the college level. He has a won/lost record of 203 wins and 227 losses at Biscayne College and 289 wins and 268 losses overall. His team won the Sunshine State Conference championship in 1982. He was selected as the Kodak District Coach of the Year, NCAA Division II, and the Co-Coach of the Year in the Sunshine State Conference in 1982.

QUICK PICK-UP DRILL

Purpose: To teach players to pick-up their offensive player quickly
Personnel and Equipment Needed: Five offensive players, five defensive players, one coach, one basketball and the entire court

Teaching Points: 1) Make sure that players communicate with each other. 2) Have players concentrate on picking up their men quickly.

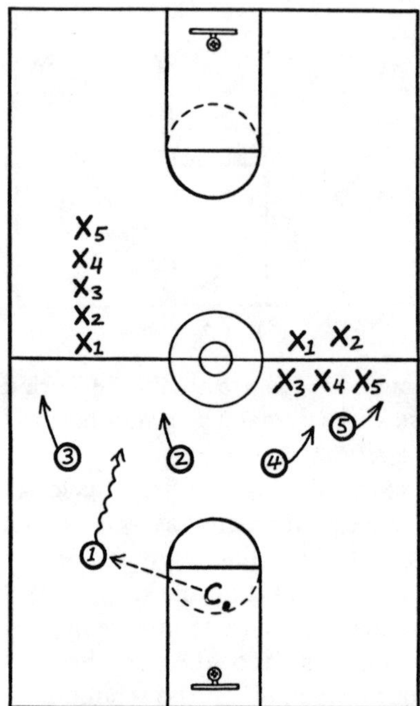

Directions: Place five defensive players (X1-X5) in various alignments. See the two examples in the diagram. The defensive players have their backs turned to the offensive players and have no idea as to how the offensive players are lined up on the floor. The coach has the ball, yells "ball," and then quickly passes to any of the offensive players. Upon hearing "ball," the defensive players immediately turn and begin calling out the names or numbers of the men they will be picking up defensively. Each defensive man points to the man he is playing and helps his teammates by asking who is playing number 24 and perhaps pushing a specific teammate in the direction of the offensive man he is to cover. The coach can change alignments after each play. The defense goes three times, then the offense becomes defense, and the defense becomes offense.

COACH DICK PARFITT—CENTRAL MICHIGAN UNIVERSITY

Coach Parfitt has been coaching for thirty-one years. Twenty-two of those thirty-one have been at the college level. He has a won/lost record of 173 wins and 145 losses at Central Michigan. His teams won the Mid-American Conference championship in 1975, 1977 and 1979. He was named Mid-American Coach of the Year in 1975.

ROLL THE BALL—GET BACK DRILL

Purpose: To teach the transition from offense to defense
Personnel and Equipment Needed: One coach or manager, a minimum of ten players, one basketball and the entire floor
Teaching Points: 1) Work hard on the offensive boards. 2) When a basket is made, sprint back to lane. 3) As the ball crosses half-court, communicate and find your defensive assignment.

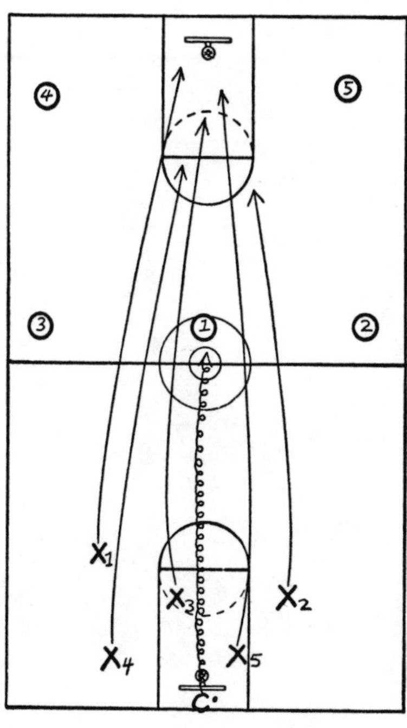

Directions: Have five players (X1-X5) run through their offensive pattern, without any defense, for a specified number of passes and then score. Have five other players (O1-O5) at the other end of the floor positioned as shown. After the shot is made, X1-X5 sprint back to the free throw lane. The coach gets the ball out of the net and rolls it to one of the players waiting at the other end (O1-O5). It is now five-on-five until a score or a turnover occurs. At that point, the two teams switch positions and they work the drill to the other end.

Part IV

FAST BREAK DRILLS

COACH MIKE POLLIO—KENTUCKY WESLEYAN COLLEGE

Coach Pollio has been coaching for eighteen years. Ten of those eighteen have been at the college level. He has a three-year won/lost record of 65 wins and 25 losses as a head coach. His team finished third in the NCAA Division II tournament. He was named Great Lakes Valley Coach of the Year in 1981 and Kodak NABC Regional Coach of the Year in 1982.

TWO-MAN FAST BREAK DRILL

Purpose: To teach the fast break, shooting on the move and conditioning

Personnel and Equipment Needed: Two coaches or managers, a minimum of four players, two basketballs, a chair or cone, a football blocking shield and the entire floor

Teaching Points: 1) Make the proper outlet pass. 2) Take the ball to the middle. 3) Wing players stay wide. 4) Emphasize the five options available to the point and the wing.

Directions: Divide your team into two groups. Have the guards line up at the hash mark and have the big men line up behind the end line near the basket. The drill begins with O1 coming onto the floor and rebounding the ball that the coach tosses off the backboard. Once he has secured the rebound, he outlets the ball to O2 who is waiting at the hash mark. O2 takes the ball to the middle on the dribble, and the rebounder (O1) fills the wing. A chair or cone is placed on the floor that he must go around to make sure he stays wide. As the two players approach the scoring area, there are five options available to them. They are: 1) the guard (O2) hits the wing (O1) for the lay up (make sure that O2 stops at the free throw line); 2) O2 pulls up for the jump shot; 3) O2 hits O1 for the jump shot (make sure the angle is correct); 4) O2 hits O1 who reverses the ball back to O2 for the jump shot; 5) O1, instead of outletting the ball, throws a lead pass to O2 and then tries to catch O2 and block his shot. The coach at the other end hinders O2 with a blocking shield.

All the players run the same options three or four times and then you can change.

After the players shoot, they can stop at that end or run the drill as a continuous drill by having O1 get the rebound, outletting it to O2 at the hash mark, and proceeding down the floor to the original end on the other side. The next two in line start when the first group shoots.

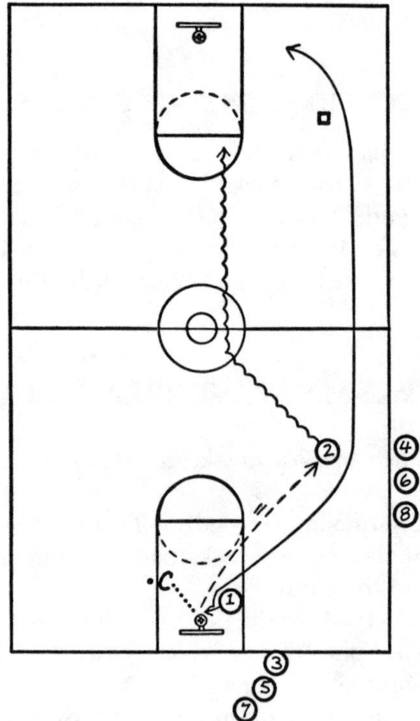

COACH STEVE YODER—UNIVERSITY OF WISCONSIN

Coach Yoder has been coaching for twenty-three years. Nine of those twenty-three have been at the college level. He has an overall won/lost record of 322 wins and 181 losses. His teams won the Mid-American Conference championship in 1982 and were co-champions in 1981. He was named MAC Coach of the Year in 1981 and 1982.

LOOSE BALL DRILL

Purpose: To develop aggressiveness and the ability to pick up the loose ball

Personnel and Equipment Needed: One coach or manager, a minimum of two players, one basketball and the entire floor
Teaching Points: 1) Be aggressive after the ball. 2) Make sure you have control of the ball before taking off to the other end. 3) When taking the ball to the basket, do so in a straight line.

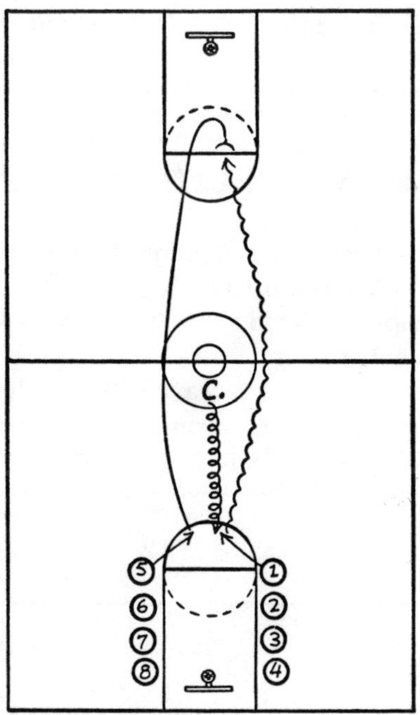

Directions: Have your players line up on either side of the free throw lane. The coach has the ball and is positioned out at the center circle. The first player in each line will be the first to go. The drill is started by the coach rolling, bouncing or throwing the ball in the air. The two players go after the loose ball. The player who comes up with the ball takes it on the dribble in a straight line to the basket. He must shoot a lay-up. The other player gets back on defense as hard as he can go and tries to stop the lay-up. After they finish, the players go to the end of the line. The coach may roll the ball anywhere on the floor.

COACH DUANE A. WOLTZEN—LAKELAND COLLEGE

Coach Woltzen has been coaching for twenty-eight years. Nineteen of those twenty-eight have been at the college level. He has compiled a won/lost record of 459 wins and 184 losses at Lakeland and 610 wins and 254 losses overall. His teams have won ten conference titles, one state championship and fifteen holiday tournaments. He was a member of the coaching staff for the World University Games in 1973 and the Pan-American Games in 1975.

THREE-MAN WEAVE—SHOOTER ON DEFENSE DRILL

Purpose: To improve passing, making the transition to defense, and handling the two-on-one fast break
Personnel and Equipment Needed: A minimum of three players, one basketball and the entire floor
Teaching Points: 1) Keep the weave wide and have players concentrate on the lay-ups. 2) Shooter sprints back on defense. 3) The non-shooters immediately rebound and start a two-on-one fast break, making good passes.

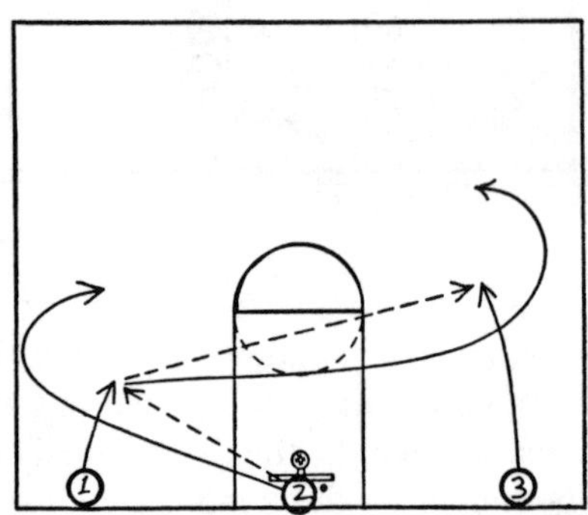

Directions: Have the players line up in three lines behind the baseline. O2 has the ball and starts the weave by passing to O1 and then going behind his pass to touch the sideline. O1 then passes to O3 and goes behind O3 to touch the sideline. O3 passes to O2 and the drill continues in this manner all the way down the floor until a lay-up is shot at the other end. Once the shot is taken, the two non-shooters rebound the ball and begin a two-on-one fast break against the defending shooter.

COACH JAMES T. VALVANO—NORTH CAROLINA STATE UNIVERSITY

Coach Valvano has been coaching for fourteen years all at the collegiate level. He has an overall won/lost record of 199 wins and 130 losses. His teams have received four NCAA post-season tournament bids. His team won the NCAA national title in 1983. He was named NCAA Division I Coach of the Year in 1983.

THREE-LINE BREAK DRILL

Purpose: To develop primary break skills and to refine the options available on the three man break

Personnel and Equipment Needed: A minimum of three players, one basketball and the entire floor

Teaching Points: 1) Make strong quick passes. 2) Concentrate on scoring at the other end. 3) Emphasize the timing between the point (dribbler) and the wingmen.

Directions: Have your players divide themselves into three lines and line up behind the baseline as diagrammed. The drill begins by having the first three players come out, in this case O1, O2, and O3. The point man O1 declares a side as in a sideline break. He may dribble up the court quickly to the free throw line extended and make the play, or he may pitch the ball ahead to the sprinting wings for lay-ups and jumpers. They execute a fast break to the other end with one of the following options:

1) the point man dribbles to the free throw line extended and passes to one of the wings for a lay-up;
2) the point man dribbles to the free throw line extended or pitches the ball ahead to one of the wings for a jumper;
3) the point man dribbles to the free throw line extended and makes a drive to the basket or takes a jumper;
4) the point man passes the ball to a wing and gets a return pass at the free throw line extended, then passes the ball to the

other wing who has gone to the baseline and flashed back to the opposite elbow for the jump shot;

5) the point man pitches the ball ahead to one of the sprinting wings. The wing who receives the ball dribbles it to the corner (to flatten out the defense) and passes it back to the point man at the elbow, who reverses the ball to the other wing at the other elbow for the jumper.

As soon as the first group is finished the next three players in line go on their three-man break.

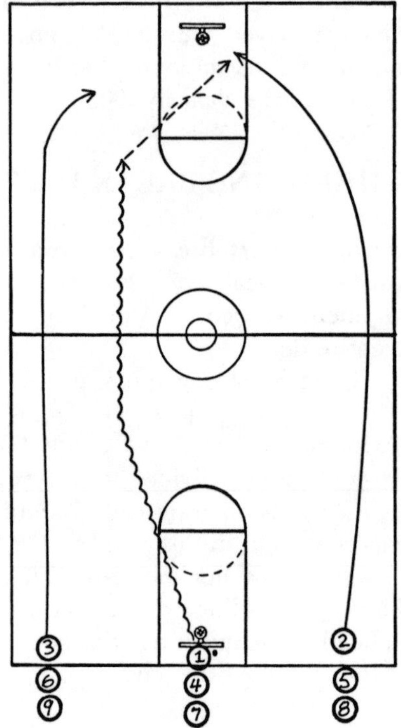

COACH SONNY ALLEN—UNIVERSITY OF NEVADA AT RENO

Coach Allen has been coaching for twenty-five years. Twenty-four of those twenty-five have been at the college level. He has an overall won/lost record of 290 wins and 206 losses. His team won the NCAA Division II championship in 1975. He was named NCAA Division II National Coach of the Year and NABC Division II Coach of the Year in 1975.

THREE-ON-NONE DRILL

Purpose: To develop dribbling and passing skills of the point man and running techniques for the wingmen
Personnel and Equipment Needed: A minimum of three players, one basketball and the entire floor
Teaching Points: 1) Emphasize the dribbling speed of the point guard. 2) Point guard should make a good pass and remain in the free throw line area. 3) Emphasize proper lane alignment of the wingmen. 4) Emphasize rebounding and outlet passes of wingmen.

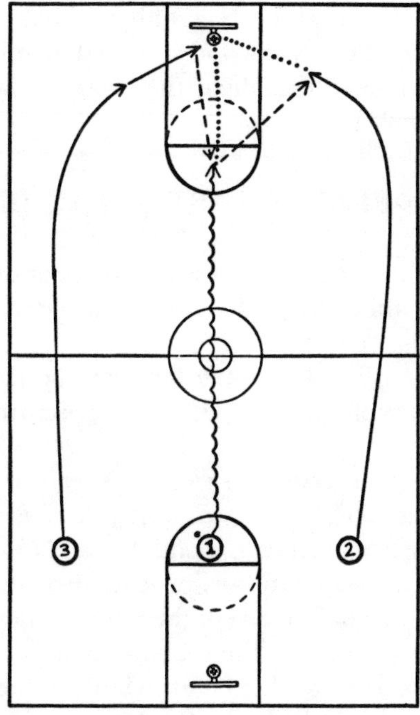

Directions: Align the first three players as shown. On the signal "go" from the point guard, the first threesome starts down the floor with the point guard dribbling the ball. He stops in the free throw line area and passes to a wingman. The non-shooting wingman rebounds the made shot and passes it back to the point guard at the free throw line area. The point guard can shoot the ball or pass it back to either wingman waiting under the basket. If the point guard shoots a jump shot and misses, the wingmen will rebound the missed shot and put it in the basket. This trio keeps shooting until two baskets are made.

To carry this drill a little further, after the second shot is made the ball is passed back to the point guard at the free throw line area. The wingmen fill the lanes and this trio fast-breaks back in the opposite direction. Only one shot is made at this end of the court.

COACH CALVIN MOSES, ASSISTANT COACH—CREIGHTON UNIVERSITY

Coach Moses has been coaching for nine years. Two of those nine have been at the college level. He has a high school won/lost record of 110 wins and 29 losses. His teams won sectional championships in 1979 and 1982. He was named Coach of the Year in the Chicago Public School League in 1982.

THREE-PLAYER FAST BREAK DRILL

Purpose: To teach filling the lanes, passing, dribbling and shooting
Personnel and Equipment Needed: A minimum of three players, one basketball and the entire floor
Teaching Points: 1) Fill the proper lanes on the fast break. 2) Make good passes while moving at top speed. 3) Concentrate and make the lay-up.
Directions: Have your players divide up evenly into three lines behind the end line. The player in the middle (O2) has the ball and dribbles to the top of the key at the other end. O1 and O3 stay wide, fill the lanes when they reach the free throw line extended, and angle in toward the basket. O2 passes the ball to one of them for the lay-up; in this case it is O3. O2 follows his pass in for the rebound and O3 and O1 cross underneath the basket and go to the opposite lane on their return trip. O2 then dribbles the ball back down the floor and feeds the ball to O1 for the lay-up.

Variation: Six players may be incorporated into this drill by having players O4, O5 and O6 start as soon as the first three players have made their turns and are headed back.

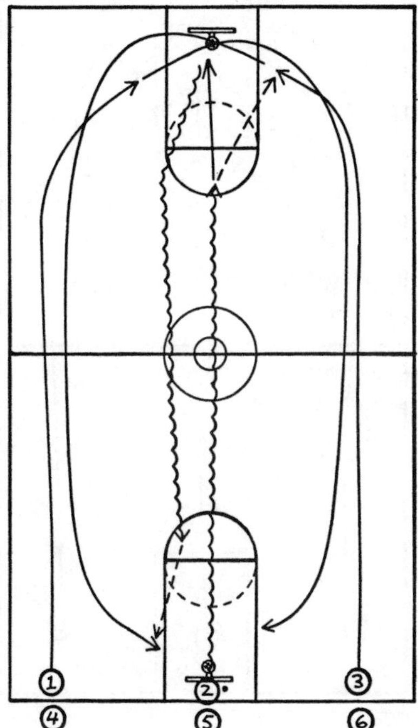

COACH SONNY SMITH—AUBURN UNIVERSITY

Coach Smith has been coaching for twenty-five years. Fourteen of those twenty-five have been at the college level. He has a won/lost record of 63 wins and 77 losses at Auburn. His team won the Ohio Valley championship in 1978. He was named Ohio Valley Conference Coach of the Year in 1978.

THREE-ON-ONE DRILL

Purpose: To teach the fundamentals of the fast break
Personnel and Equipment Needed: A minimum of four players, one basketball and the entire floor
Teaching Points: 1) Emphasize good ball handling and passing. 2) How to handle the three-on-one break. 3) Execute a good baseball pass.

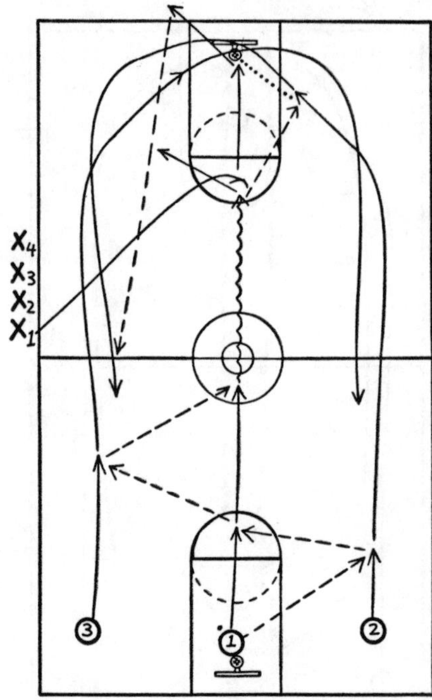

Directions: Have your team line up in four lines. The first line at half-court should be all big men. The other three lines can be made up of the remaining players and should be out of bounds behind the end line. The drill begins with the first three players (O1, O2 and O3) taking the ball to the other end in a fast break. The defensive man (X1) moves on the floor at half-court and defends against the break. After the offense scores, the defender takes the ball out of bounds, sets his feet and throws a baseball pass to either O2 or O3. O2 and O3 crossed under the basket after the score and are sprinting up the sidelines looking for the pass. O1 will break out to the short outlet in case X1 chooses to pass to him instead. He would then pass it on to O2 or O3. After the pass is complete, three more come out to continue the drill and a new defender comes out at half-court.

COACH DAVID "SMOKEY" GAINES—SAN DIEGO STATE UNIVERSITY

Coach Gaines has been coaching for thirteen years. Ten of those thirteen have been at the college level. He has an overall won/lost record of 106 wins and 62 losses as a head coach in six years. He has led one of his teams to an NCAA Division I post-season tournament.

CONTINUOUS FAST BREAK DRILL

Purpose: To teach fast break options
Personnel and Equipment Needed: A minimum of fifteen players, one basketball and the entire floor
Teaching Points: Offense: 1) wings stay wide to spread the defense; 2) make good passes but do not over-pass; 3) have good shot selection. Defense: 1) find your man quickly; 2) put pressure on the ball.

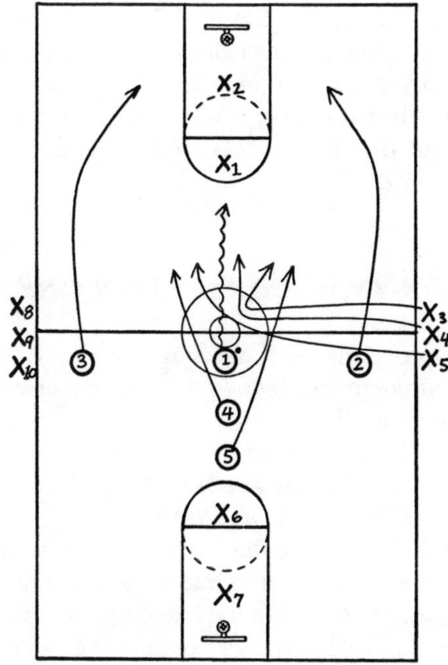

Directions: Divide the players into three groups of five each. O1, O2, O3, O4 and O5 start in the middle of the floor, with two players, X1 and X2, in tandem at one end of the floor, and two players, X6 and X7, in tandem at the other end. The remaining players, X3, X4 and X5, and X8, X9 and X10, gather at opposite sides of the court at the midcourt line as shown above. The drill begins with O1, O2, O3, O4 and O5 attacking X1 and X2. Once the ball crosses the midcourt line, X3, X4 and

X5 begin action by touching the center circle and then picking up their offensive man and guard him until they gain possession.

Note: If the offense scores and gets the ball out of the net before the defense, they set up to score again at the same basket. Once X1, X2, X3, X4 and X5 gain possession, they attack X6, X7, X8, X9 and X10 at the opposite end of the floor. The drill is continuous and ends after a pre-arranged time is complete.

COACH JOHNNY ORR—IOWA STATE UNIVERSITY

Coach Orr has been in coaching thirty-three years. Twenty-four of those thirty-three have been at the college level. He has an overall collegiate won/lost record of 288 wins and 185 losses. His teams won the Big Ten Conference title in 1974 and 1977. He was named Big Ten Coach of the Year in 1974 and 1976 and NCAA Division I National Coach of the Year in 1976 and 1977.

THREE-ON-TWO AND TWO-ON-ONE DRILL

Purpose: To improve the skills necessary for the transition game
Personnel and Equipment Needed: A minimum of seven players, one basketball and the entire floor
Teaching Points: 1) Outside fast break lanes stay wide. 2) Make good cuts. 3) Middle man stops at the free throw line. 4) Two-on-one should stay wide and pass the ball back and forth.
Directions: Have the players align themselves as shown. If you have more than seven players, they should line up behind O6 and O7. O1, O2 and O3 begin the drill by bringing the ball down in a three-on-two situation against X4 and X5. The shooter becomes the defensive man on the return trip down the floor. After the shot, if X4 or X5 gets the rebound or they have been scored upon, they bring the ball back down the floor against the first shooter (in this case O2). When they score or O2 gets the rebound, O2 continues the drill and is joined by O6 and O7 as he breaks to the other end to go against O1 and O3 who have stayed and become the new defense. X4 and X5 go to the end of the line. This drill can continue in this manner for as long as you like.

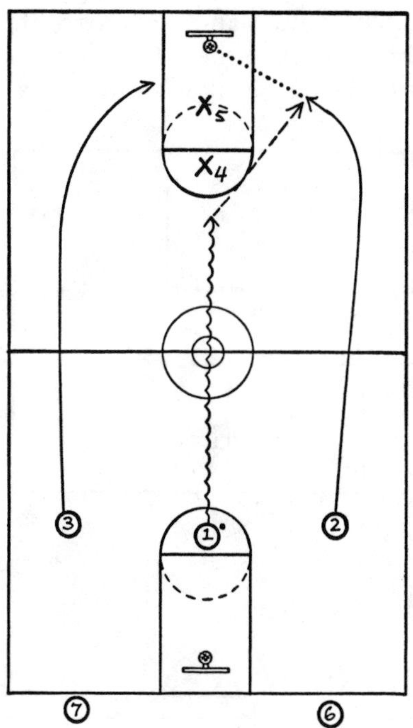

COACH BILL FRIEDER—UNIVERSITY OF MICHIGAN

Coach Frieder has coached at the University of Michigan for eleven years. Four of those eleven have been as the head coach. He has an overall won/lost record at Michigan of 59 wins and 54 losses. His teams have made two National Invitational Tournament appearances and won the NIT in 1984.

THREE-ON-TWO WITH A CHASER DRILL

Purpose: To teach fast break situations both offensively and defensively

Personnel and Equipment Needed: A coach or a manager, a minimum of twelve players, two basketballs and the entire floor

Teaching Points: Defensively: 1) stopping the initial break, utilizing a tandem set; 2) matching up man-to-man once the initial break has been stopped; 3) hustling back in the transition to defense. Offensively: 1) taking advantage of the fast break when you have a man advantage.

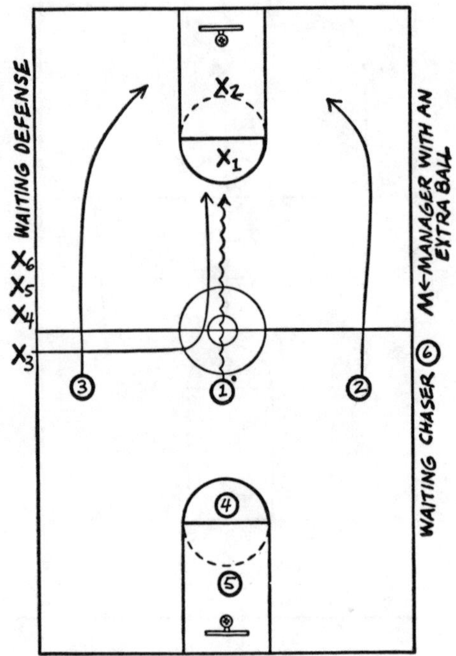

Directions: Divide the twelve players into two teams of six with opposite colored jerseys on. The first three offensive men (O1, O2 and O3) take the ball down the floor against the two waiting defensive men (X1 and X2). The third defensive man (X3) at half-court is designated as the chaser. When the ball passes half-court, the chaser runs onto the court, touches the center jump circle, and continues in to join the action. The action continues at that basket until the offense scores, or the defense gains possession by a turnover or a rebound. Any turnover results in the defense gaining possession. Upon gaining possession, the three that were on defense now become the three on offense and push the ball up the floor. The next three waiting on the "O" side (O4, O5 and O6) are now on defense at the opposite end.

The action is continual, never stopping for anything, including fouls. After an offensive team has lost possession, it then returns to its original side of the floor (running up the sideline, out-of-bounds, so to not interfere with the action) to assume defense on the next possession coming their way. Score may be kept to add a fun, competitive element to the drill.

COACH PETER DEES—BERRY COLLEGE

Coach Dees has been coaching for nine years. Seven of those nine have been at the college level. He has an overall won/lost record of 125 wins and 93 losses. His team won the Georgia Junior College Southern Conference title in 1974. He was named Kentucky Junior College Co-Coach of the Year in 1973.

CATCH-UP DRILL

Purpose: To teach the skills involved in running the fast break and defending against it

Personnel and Equipment Needed: Two coaches or managers, a minimum of six players, one basketball and the entire floor.

Teaching Points: 1) Emphasize making contact on the block out. 2) Make a good outlet pass. 3) Get the ball to the middle after the outlet. 4) Defense needs to make the transition from offense to defense quickly.

Directions: Have the players get in groups of three and line up behind the end line. Now have one group of three come out on offense and one group come out on defense. The coach has the ball and starts the drill by tossing the ball up on the board. The defensive team blocks off their respective offensive players and secures the rebound. The offensive team crashes the board for the offensive rebound and the player whose name is called out by the coach must run and touch the baseline before he can retreat to the other end and play defense. Once the rebound is secured by the defense, they take it to the other end in a three-man break. The two offensive players whose names were not called must sprint back and defend against that three-man break until their teammate catches up. The drill continues until there is a score, a turnover or a rebound. Then the ball is given to the coach at that end and the teams come back in the same manner.

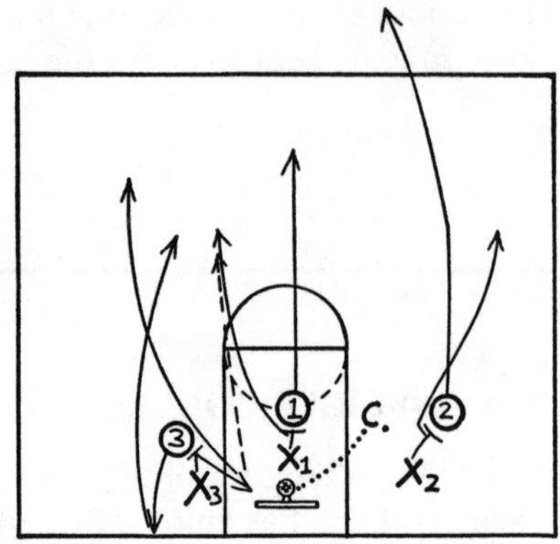

COACH IVAN SCHULER—ROBERTS WESLEYAN COLLEGE

Coach Schuler has been coaching for twenty-two years. Thirteen of those twenty-two have been at the college level as either an assistant or a head coach. While he was an assistant at Biola University for seven years their teams won at least 20 games a year.

PIT DRILL

Purpose: To improve offensive and defensive skills related to the fast break

Personnel and Equipment Needed: A minimum of eight players, one basketball and the entire floor

Teaching Points: 1) Catch and look when receiving a pass. 2) Make a good baseball pass to half-court. 3) If the middle is congested, you need to square out on the ball side. 4) Emphasize a good tandem defense.

Directions: Align your players as shown. O1 works one-on-one against X3 (check defensive and offensive skills). If O1 scores, X3 takes the ball out of the net and steps out of bounds to make a baseball pass to half-court to O2. If O1 does not score and X3 rebounds the ball, he makes a good outlet pass to O2 at half-court. O5 slides over to the center circle to receive a pass from O2. O4 fills the third lane of the fast break. X1 challenges the dribbler, forcing him to one side. X2 takes the first pass and X1 drops back to intercept the cross-court pass. O5 steps in the

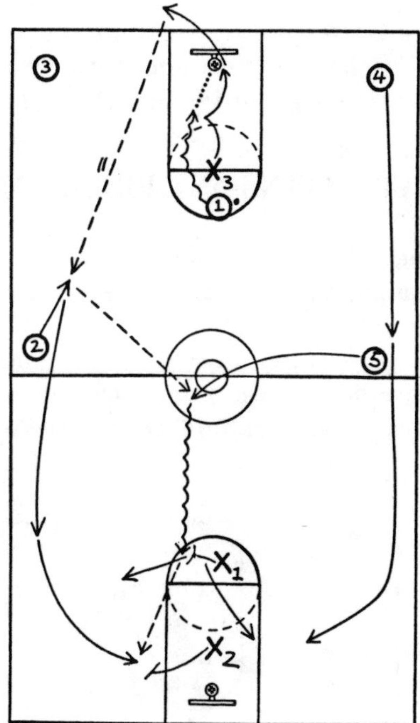

direction of his pass with his hands up for the return pass and a one-hand jump shot. O4 waits at a good angle until the shot goes up or for a return pass from O5. The players in the four corner spots will rotate clockwise after each outlet. After a make or a miss at the end of the fast break, the ball is thrown to half-court and then back into the pit for a new one-on-one. Each player in the pit goes two times on offense and defense before two new players rotate into the pit. The tandem at the defensive end become the new pit players.

COACH DICK DANIELSON—UNIVERSITY OF PITTSBURG AT BEDFORD

Coach Danielson has been coaching for twenty-three years. Eight of those twenty-three have been at the college level. He has a won/lost record of 149 wins and 57 losses at the University of Pittsburg. His team won the Penn York Conference title in 1977 and 1979. He was named NAIA District 18 Coach of the Year and Pittsburgh Press Coach of the Year for Pennsylvania colleges in Western Pennsylvania in 1982.

ELEVEN-MAN FAST BREAK DRILL

Purpose: To teach all aspects of the fast break
Personnel and Equipment Needed: A minimum of eleven players, one basketball, and the entire floor
Teaching Points: Offense: 1) stay wide in the lanes; 2) cut at a 45-degree angle at the free throw line extended. Defense: 1) take the offensive charge; 2) box out for rebounds; 3) make a proper outlet pass.

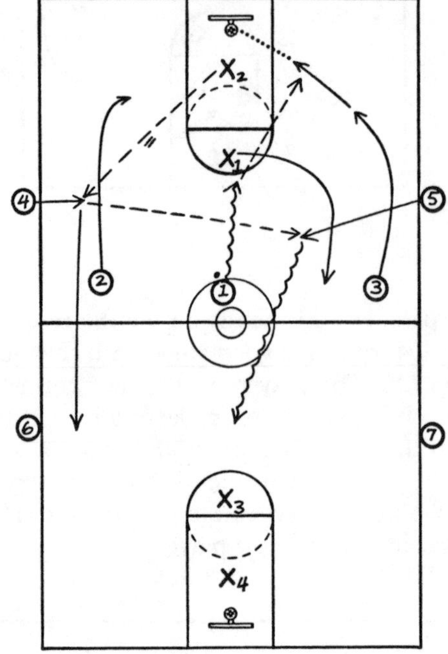

Directions: The eleven players align themselves as shown. If you have more players, they fill in at the spots on the sideline. The X's represent defensive players and they are set in tandem at both ends of the floor. The drill begins with O1 dribbling the ball toward the left goal while O2 and O3 stay wide and make a 45-degree cut at the free throw line extended. O1 looks to pass to either O2 or O3 when he reaches the top of the circle. After the pass is made, O1 takes two steps in the direction of the pass, pulls up and becomes an outlet for a return pass from either O2 or O3.

The ball remains alive until someone scores or the defense gains position. After the ball is secured by the defense, the outlet is made to the side of the floor where the ball is recovered to the man who is at the front of the line, in this case O4. The opposite outlet man (O5) moves toward the ball for a pass from O4 and becomes the middle man in the break. The defensive man, who did not rebound the ball, then fills the third lane. The shooter and rebounder go to the ends of the opposite line on the sideline and the other two offensive players become the new defense. When the ball is in the middle, it is dribbled down the floor with the outside lanes filled and the drill continues in this manner up and down the floor as long as you like.

COACH DON BRUBACHER—TABOR COLLEGE

Coach Brubacher has been coaching for seven years all at the college level. He has an overall won/lost record of 92 wins and 68 losses. His team won the KCAC championship in 1982 and were co-champions in 1981. He was selected KCAC Coach of the Year in 1981 and 1982.

ELEVEN-MAN FAST BREAK WITH A DEFENSIVE TRAILER DRILL

Purpose: To develop fast break techniques
Personnel and Equipment Needed: A minimum of twelve players, one basketball and the entire floor
Teaching Points: 1) Block out on the boards. 2) Outlet man create a passing lane to the ball. 3) Wings run the sideline to the top of the key and cut to the basket. 4) Take the first good shot to take advantage of the mismatch.
Directions: First, have two players form a tandem defense at each end of the floor. Next, have three players come out on offense to attack one of the tandems. Finally, have the remaining players divide themselves up into the five sideline spots shown. The drill begins with the three offensive players attacking one of the tandems. As soon as the ball or dribbler passes half-court, the third defensive man, who is standing

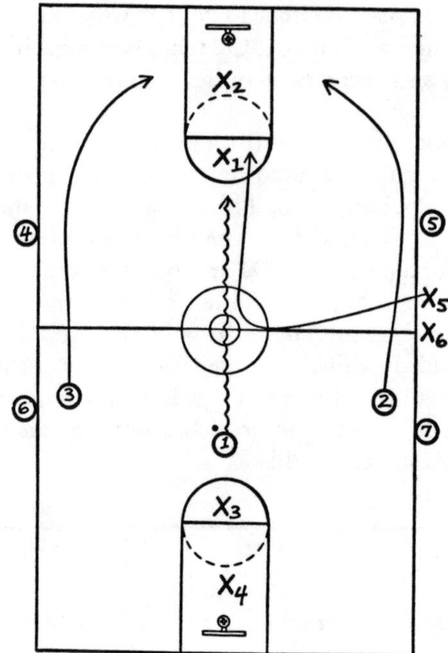

out of bounds at half-court, sprints to the center circle, touches it with his foot and enters into defense against the break. The rebounder or the player who retrieves the ball after a made basket makes the outlet pass to one of the two wings and follows his pass to fill the lane. The wing who receives the pass takes it to the middle on the dribble and the drill continues to the other end. The remaining players fill the open spots in the tandem and on the sidelines.

COACH GEORGE WAGGONER—ST. JOSEPH'S COLLEGE

Coach Waggoner has been coaching for seventeen years. Nine of those seventeen have been at the college level. He has a collegiate won/lost record of 132 wins and 109 losses. His teams won the Great Lakes Valley Conference title in 1979 and the Hoosier-Buckeye Conference in 1976. He was named Coach of the Year in 1972, 1976, 1978 and 1979.

ELEVEN-MAN FAST BREAK PUMA STYLE DRILL

Purpose: To teach the fundamentals of the puma fast break
Personnel and Equipment Needed: A minimum of eleven players, one basketball and the entire floor
Teaching Points: 1) Only the guards handle the ball on the break. 2) Wing men cross underneath the basket and do not stop and beg for the ball. 3) Teach good ball movement after the initial thrust.

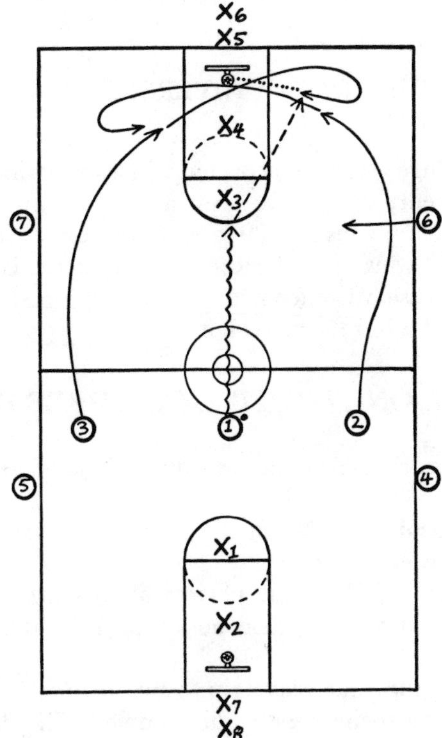

Directions: Have your guards line up at the hash marks and your forwards and centers line up underneath each basket. Two of the forwards and centers at each end step out to play defense and will become the wing men. The drill is started by a guard taking the ball in the middle and a forward or center filling each lane. The guard stops at the free throw line, the wing men make a 45-degree angle cut for the basket at the free throw line extended and cross underneath the basket and hook for a 15-foot jumper. The point guard moves to the side of the lane he passes to. They try to score without dribbling after the first pass is made by passing the ball side to side. When the defense gets the ball (rebound or interception) the next guard at the hash mark moves to the top of the key to start the break the other way. The two defensive players fill the lanes on the break the other way. The original offensive players go to the ends of their respective lines.

COACH BILL MULLIGAN—UNIVERSITY OF CALIFORNIA AT IRVINE

Coach Mulligan has been coaching for twenty-three years. Seventeen of those twenty-three have been at the college level. He has a won/lost record of 56 wins and 29 losses at the University of California at Irvine and 388 wins and 147 losses overall at the college level. His teams won the Mission Conference championship in 1977, 1978, 1979, 1980 and received a bid to the NIT in 1982.

THREE-ON-TWO/FIVE-ON-THREE DRILL

Purpose: To teach players how to fill designated lanes on the fast break

Personnel and Equipment Needed: A minimum of ten players, one basketball and the entire floor

Teaching Points: 1)Have the players fill designated lanes. 2) Rebound the ball and make a good outlet. 3) Take the first good shot available.

Directions: Divide your players into two teams (O's and X's) and have them position themselves as diagrammed. The drill begins with O1, O4 and O5 attacking O2 and O3 in a three-on-two break. After one shot, made or missed, they get the ball and get it to O1. If they scored, O5 inbounds the ball to O1. These five players take the ball to the other end against X4 and X5. As the ball crosses half-court, X1 is allowed to come on defense by touching the center circle and then going after the ball. When X4, X5 and X1 get the ball (via a steal, turnover, rebound or score) they attack X2 and X3 who enter in tandem while O1, O2, O3, O4 and O5 are attacking X4, X5 and X1. The O's then go to the five positions that the five X's occupied at the start of the drill.

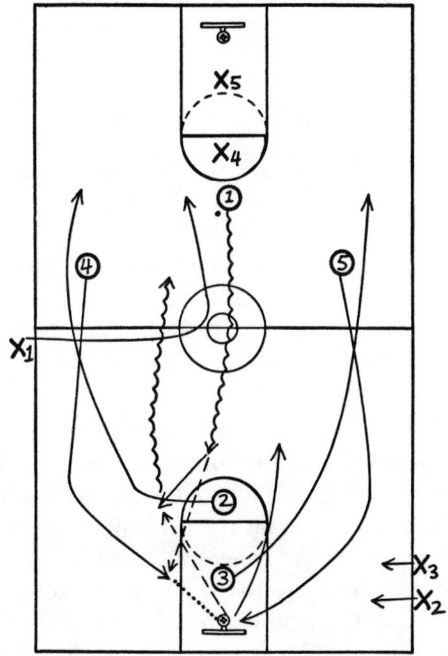

COACH JIM MORRIS—INDIANA UNIVERSITY SOUTHEAST

Coach Morris has been coaching for twenty-five years. Twelve of those twenty-five have been at the college level. He has an overall won/lost record of 278 wins and 288 losses. His teams have won several district, regional and sectional championships in both Kentucky and Indiana. He also coached a team that won the Kentucky State high school championship. He was named Kentucky High School Coach of the Year in 1960, Louisville High School Coach of the Year in 1961 and Indiana High School District Coach of the Year in 1967.

FOUR-MAN BREAK DRILL

Purpose: To teach how to outlet the ball and fill the lanes
Personnel and Equipment Needed: A minimum of four players, one basketball and the entire floor
Teaching Points: 1) Time your jump and rebound the ball at the peak. 2) Make a good overhead outlet pass. 3) Fill the proper lanes on the break.

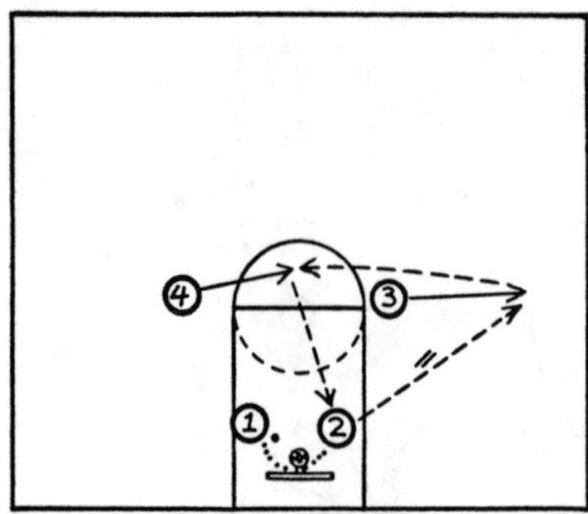

Directions: Players O1 and O2 line up on either side of the basket and players O3 and O4 on either side of the lane at the free throw line as shown. O1 has the ball and begins the drill by throwing the ball off the backboard and over the basket, where O2 rebounds it. O2 turns to the outside and makes an outlet pass to O3 who has stepped out to the outlet area. O3 then passes to O4 who has filled the middle. O4 passes to O2 who starts the drill over again by throwing the ball off the backboard and over the basket to O1. O1 rebounds the ball, turns to the outside, and makes an outlet pass to O4. O4 passes the ball to O3 who has come to the middle. The drill can continue in this manner as long as desired.

Variation: To practice the full-court break, the coach shouts, "go", and the players break to the other end. O3 and O4 fill the two lanes, the offside forward gets the open lane and the rebounder is the trailer. The ball can be advanced down the side or up the middle.

COACH KEVIN O'NEILL—MARYCREST COLLEGE

Coach O'Neill has been coaching for four years. Three of those four have been at the college level. He has an overall won/lost record of 43 wins and 34 losses.

TOUCH-AND-GO DRILL

Purpose: To teach the skills involved in the fast break
Personnel and Equipment Needed: One coach or manager, a minimum of ten players, one basketball and the entire floor

Teaching Points: 1) To make the transition from offense to defense and vice versa. 2) Excellent way to teach the secondary break. 3) Emphasize good passes and good shot selection.

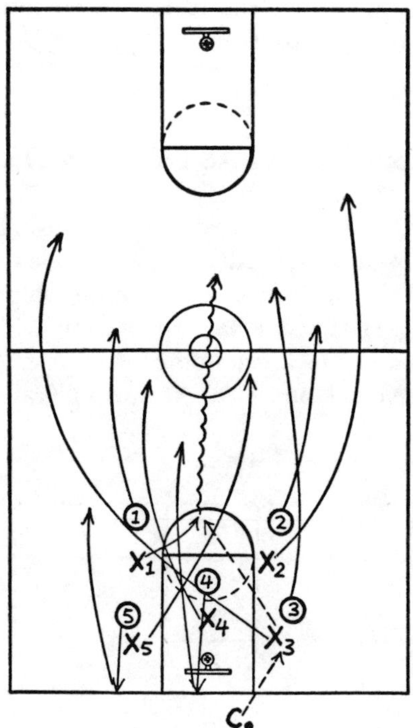

Directions: Have your players divide up into two teams and align themselves as shown. The coach or manager begins the drill by passing the ball to X3. X1, X2, X3, X4 and X5 take the ball down on the fast break. O4 and O5 must touch the baseline before they can enter in on defense. This gives the fast break a true game situation. O3, O1 and O2 can do anything they like to stop the break. If the "X" team scores they will keep the ball and run the drill back the other direction. They also get two points. If they are fouled, they get one point and keep the ball. If they miss and the "O" team rebounds the ball, they bring it back the other direction and try to score. If they do, they keep possession. You can play this game to 12 points.

COACH GEORGE H. PALKE, JR.—BETHEL COLLEGE

Coach Palke has been coaching for eighteen years. Six of those eighteen have been at the college level. He has an overall won/lost record of 210 wins and 165 losses.

THREE-TEAM FAST BREAK DRILL

Purpose: To develop the skills necessary to finish a fast break
Personnel and Equipment Needed: One coach, a minimum of twelve players, one basketball, two cones and the entire floor
Teaching Points: 1) Outside lane men stay wide. (Hit the hash mark). 2) Middle man stops at the top of the circle. 3) Wings cut from the hash mark to the block on a straight line. 4) Trailer go to the block.

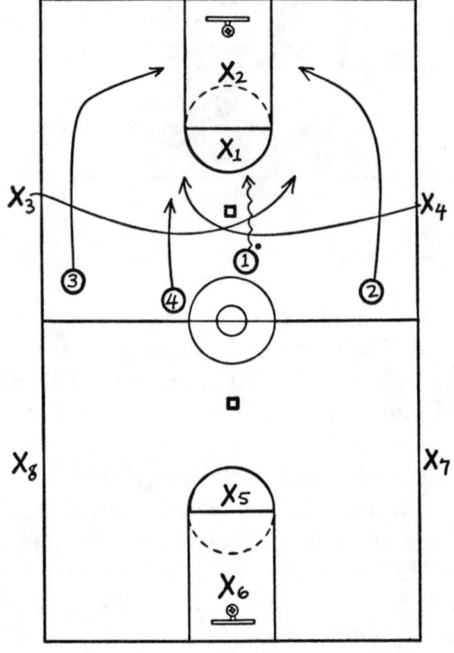

Directions: Divide the twelve players into three teams of four each (two colors and skins). Have two of the teams line up on defense at opposite ends of the court. Put two defensive men in the lane and the other two out of bounds at the hash marks. The third team has the ball on the fast break and they go in for the score. The two defensive men who are out of bounds can enter play as soon as a man from the offensive team or the ball passes them. They must go around the cone before going on defense. The drill can be run so that if you score you keep possession, or the defensive team gains possession after the score. In either case, immediately after the score the team getting the ball takes it out of bounds and fast-breaks to the opposite end. If the team on defense obtains possession without being scored upon, they fast-break to the opposite end. If the ball goes out of bounds in the front court and it belongs to the offensive team, those two teams on that end will play only half-court until there is a score or a change of possession. All fouls count as a score and the team fouled takes the ball to the opposite end on the break. This can be a competitive drill if the score is kept. You should spend about ten minutes on it.

Variation: You can make this a conversion drill by having the team that scores immediately put a full-court press on the team taking the ball out of bounds. They press to the hash marks or the midcourt line.

COACH BOB CHIPMAN—WASHBURN UNIVERSITY

Coach Chipman has been coaching for four years all at the college level. He has an overall won/lost record of 81 wins and 36 losses. His team has won the NAIA District 10 championship. He has been named KBCA College Coach of the Year.

ROTATION FIVE-MAN DRILL

Purpose: To teach the five positions on the fast break
Personnel and Equipment Needed: A minimum of five players, one basketball and the entire floor
Teaching Points: 1) Make a good outlet pass. 2) Get the ball to the middle by passing. 3) Wings stay wide. 4) Make sure the five spots get filled.

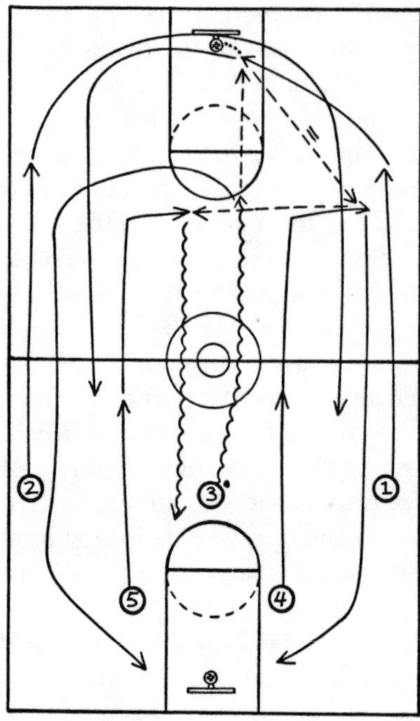

Directions: The five players position themselves on the floor as shown. O3 has the ball and he advances it down the floor on the dribble. O1 and O2 are on the wings, stay wide, and will angle to the basket when they get to the free throw line extended. O4 is the trailer and O5 is the safety. When O3 reaches the free throw line he will pass the ball to O1. O1 takes the ball in for the lay-up, continues on, and will be the trailer on the way back. O2 also looks for a pass from O3, in this case, he will not get the pass but will rebound O1's lay-up. He then will make an outlet pass to O4 to start the break back down the floor. O2 will then be the safety on the return trip. O3 passes to either O1 or O2 and goes opposite to the way he passes. He will be filling a lane on the return trip. O4 is the trailer, he slides in the direction the ball has been passed, and will be the outlet man for the return trip back down the floor. O5, who is the safety, will become the middle man on the return trip.

COACH MEL MYERS—BRIDGEWATER COLLEGE

Coach Myers has been coaching for thirty-two years. Twenty-two of those thirty-two have been at the college level at Bridgewater College.

The dean of the Old Dominion Athletic Conference coaches, he has a won/lost record of 378 wins and 351 losses at Bridgewater. His 1983–84 team finished second in the Old Dominion Athletic Conference with a 16–9 record. He was named ODAC Coach of the Year and College Division (II and III) Coach of the Year in Virginia by the state's sports information directors in 1984.

EAGLE FAST BREAK DRILL

Purpose: To teach the fundamentals of the transition game
Personnel and Equipment Needed: One coach, a minimum of ten players, one basketball and the entire floor
Teaching Points: 1) Properly block your man off the board. 2) Get to your fast break lane as quickly as possible. 3) Execute a good three-on-two break.

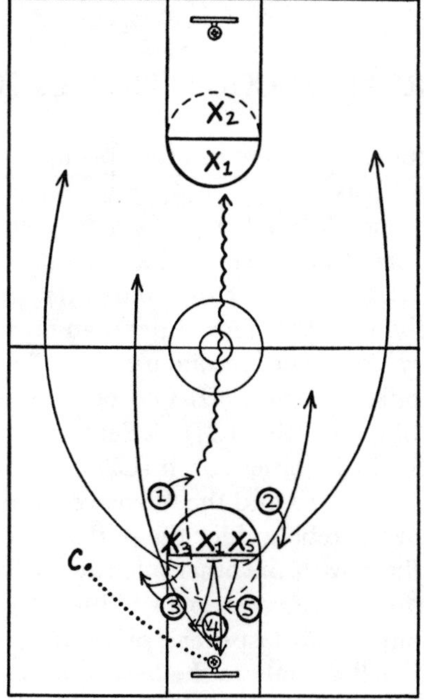

Directions: Divide the ten players into two teams, one on offense and one on defense. Have the players position themselves as diagrammed. Three defensive players are at one end, the other two at the other end. All five offensive players form a circle around the three defensive players. The coach has the ball and has the offensive players make defensive slides around the circle either to the right or to the left. When he shoots the ball, the offensive players block off the three defensive players and begin a break to the other end. The three defensive players must try to crash the board. The offensive players get to their proper lanes after they block out and the ball is secured. They then face the tandem defense at the other end. Once the offense has scored, have the teams switch and run the drill back the other way.

COACH WAYNE EARHARDT—WOFFORD COLLEGE

Coach Earhardt has been coaching for twelve years. Eight of those twelve have been at the college level. His 1980–81 team finished with a 19–11 record and that same year he was named NAIA District 6 Coach of the Year.

BREAK RECOGNITION DRILL

Purpose: To recognize when to run the "primary break" and when to run the "secondary break"
Personnel and Equipment Needed: Two coaches, a minimum of ten players, one basketball and the entire floor
Teaching Points: 1) Make sure that the outlet man goes to the side where the ball is rebounded. 2) This outlet man must recognize whether to run the "primary break" or "secondary break."
Directions: An offensive team (O1-O5) positions itself at one end of the floor with one of the coaches (C1). A defensive team (X1-X5) waits along the sideline with the other coach (C2). The drill begins with C1 tossing the ball off the board and the offensive team rebounding it. O1 breaks to the side of the rebound for the outlet pass. He then advances the ball down the floor, with the other offensive players filling the lanes and carrying out the fast break responsibilities that the coach has assigned them according to his fast break philosophy. O1 must recognize whether to take the ball directly to the basket, as on a "primary break" where the offense has the advantage, or go directly into a "secondary break" by dribbling the ball to the free throw line extended area. The "recognition" comes from the number of defensive players that C2 sends out to defend against the break. The rule is:

1) if O1 sees two or less defenders, he runs the "primary break";
2) if O1 sees three or more defenders, he runs the "secondary break." The "primary break" is the normal two-on-one or three-on-two break. The "secondary break" is a set, patterned break.

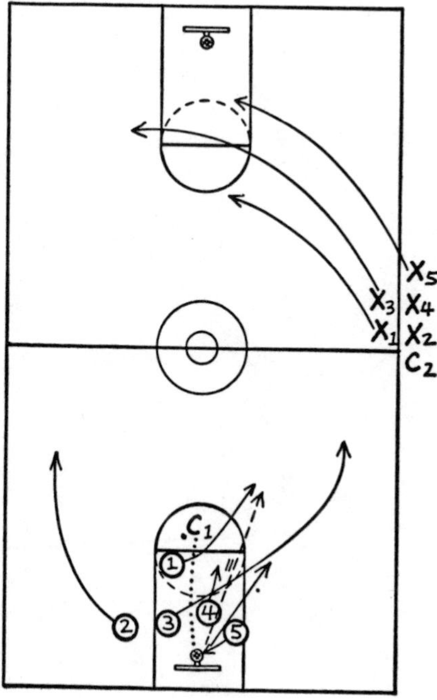

Part V

INDIVIDUAL DEVELOPMENT DRILLS

COACH HANK RAYMONDS—MARQUETTE UNIVERSITY

Coach Raymonds has been coaching for thirty-two years twenty-seven of those thirty-two have been at the college level. He has a won/lost record of 120 wins and 50 losses at Marquette and 237 wins and 97 losses overall at the collegiate level in twelve years. His teams won three NAIA District 27 titles in six years. He was named Coach of the Year in 1979 by Medalist Sports Education.

BODY CONTROL DRILL

Purpose: To help players acquire better balance and control of their bodies
Personnel and Equipment Needed: An unlimited number of players and the entire floor
Teaching Points: See Directions.

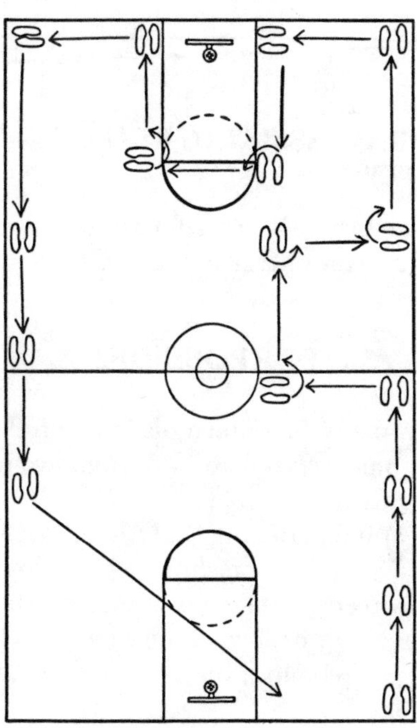

Directions: Have your players line up behind the end line. Start with an onside or crossover step, then sprint up the sideline to the free throw line extended and come to a jump stop. Then continue up the sideline to the hash mark and either jump stop or stride stop. Continue to half-court where you will change direction by hitting on the right foot and going left toward the center circle. At the center circle, reverse-pivot on your right foot and go forward to the hash mark and reverse-pivot on your right foot again. Sprint ahead to the sideline and reverse-pivot on your left foot. Then sprint to the corner and change direction by hitting on the right foot and going left. Go to the free throw lane and change direction again by hitting on the right foot and going left up the lane. Sprint to the elbow and make a reverse pivot on the right foot. Sprint along free throw line to the opposite elbow and make another reverse pivot on your right foot. Sprint down the free throw lane and at the end line make a change of direction by hitting on the right foot and going left to the corner. At the corner make another change of direction by hitting on the right foot and going left up the sideline. Come to a jump stop at the hash mark. Then sprint to half-court and come to a jump stop again. Continue up the sideline to the next hash mark and change direction by hitting on the right foot and sprinting in to the end of the line.

COACH GREG BERRY, ASSISTANT COACH—NEW MEXICO STATE UNIVERSITY

Coach Berry has been coaching for thirteen years. Nine of those thirteen have been at New Mexico State University as an assistant coach.

ALL PURPOSE DRILL

Purpose: To teach many fundamentals in one full court drill
Personnel and Equipment Needed: A minimum of eight players, three basketballs and the entire floor
Teaching Points: 1) Ball handling dexterity. 2) Defensive rebounding and outlet passing. 3) Dribbling techniques, passing and offensive rebounding. 4) Setting screens, using screens' offensive moves and shooting
Directions: O2 cuts high or low as the shooter O4 releases the ball. O2 is not attempting to rebound, but only forcing the defender to use

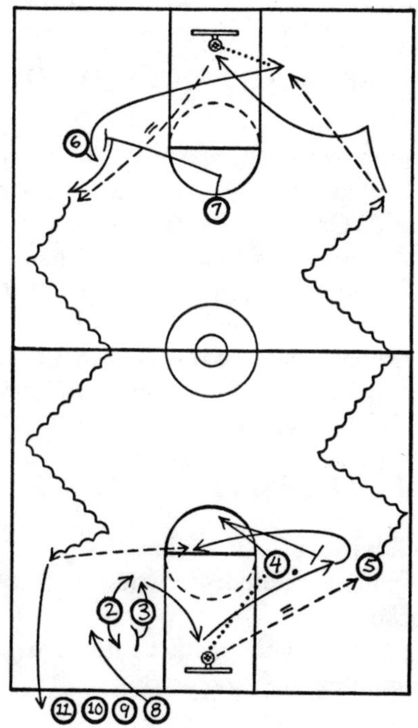

the proper pivot. O3 pivots in the appropriate direction, rebounds and outlets the ball to O5. O5 dribbles down the court changing directions three times: the first time he uses a crossover dribble, the second time he uses a spin dribble and the third time he uses a behind-the-back dribble. At the free throw line extended he stops and passes to O6 who is cutting off O7's screen. O6 may cut high for a facing move or low for a post move. After the pass, O5 moves to the offensive board by either cutting high toward the lane and reverse-pivoting toward the basket or by cutting toward the baseline and reversing into the lane. If the shot is missed, he rebounds it and puts it back in. He takes the ball out of the net and outlets it to O7 who screened for O6 coming across the lane. The shooter becomes the next screener. O7 uses the dribble techniques down the sideline, then passes the ball to O3 who is coming off O4's screen for the shot.

The rotation of players is as follows: O8 replaces O2, O2 replaces O3, O3 replaces O4, O4 replaces O5, O5 replaces O6, O6 replaces O7 and O7 goes to the end of the line.

COACH BILL FOSTER—UNIVERSITY OF SOUTH CAROLINA

Coach Bill Foster has been coaching at the collegiate level for twenty-three years. He has a won/lost record of 53 wins and 34 losses at the University of South Carolina and 374 wins and 223 losses overall. His teams won the Atlantic Coast Conference championship once and the ACC tournament championship twice. His 1978 Duke University team finished second in the nation behind Kentucky. He was named Atlantic Coast Conference Coach of the Year in 1978 and National Co-Coach of the Year by the National Association of Basketball Coaches in 1978.

TWO-MAN OFFENSIVE MANEUVER DRILLS

Purpose: To teach basic offensive skills
Personnel and Equipment Needed: A minimum of two players, one basketball and a basket
Teaching Points: 1) Do all the drills to the right and to the left. 2) Work on your ball handling and footwork.

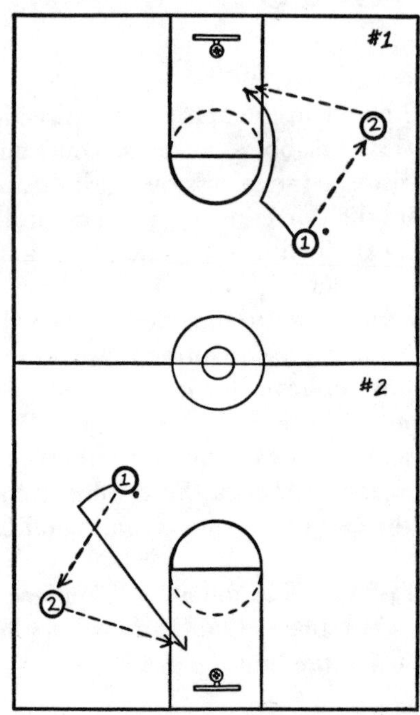

Directions: Diagram #1: O1 has the ball and passes it to O2. He then takes a step or two to his left, pushes off on his left foot and cuts to the basket to receive a pass back from O2.

Diagram #2: O1 has the ball and passes it to O2. He then takes two or three steps toward O2 (as if to set a screen for him) and cuts off his right foot to the basket for a return pass from O2.

Diagram #3: O1 has the ball and passes it to O2. O1 starts toward O2's defensive man. Then he drops behind O2 for a return pass and takes a shot over the screen.

Diagram #4: O1 has the ball and passes it to O2. O1 follows the pass as in Diagram #3 and receives the ball back from O2. O1 fakes the shot and drives off of O2's screen.

Diagram #5: O1 has the ball and passes it to O2. O1 follows the pass as in the two previous diagrams and receives the ball back from O2. O1 fakes the shot and drives off of O2's screen; O2 rolls, facing the ball, and gets a return pass from O1.

Diagram #6: O1 has the ball and passes it to O2. O1 follows the pass and sets an inside screen for O2. O2 drives off of the screen.

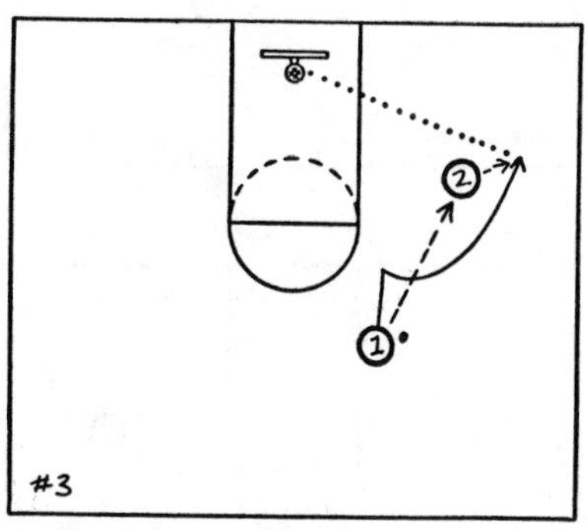

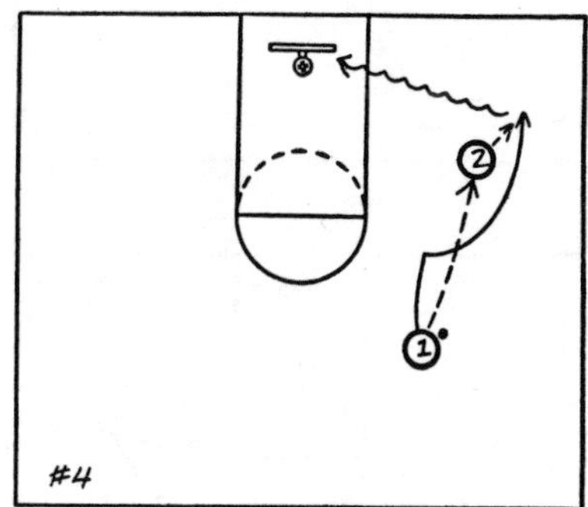

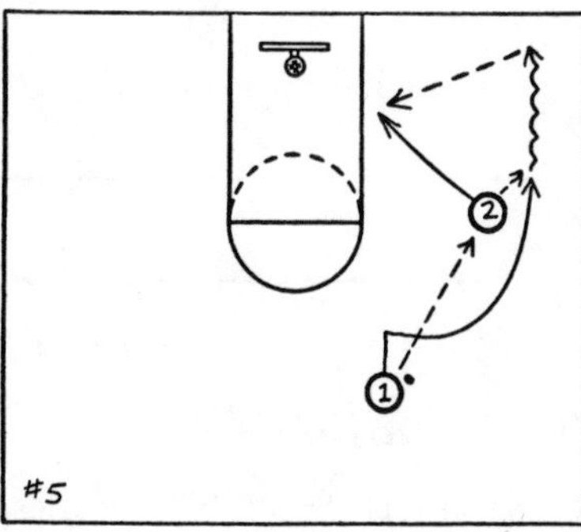

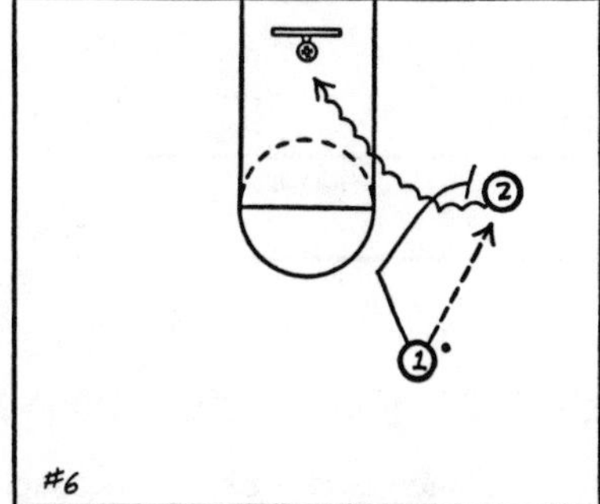

Diagram #7: O1 has the ball and passes it to O2. O1 follows the pass and sets an inside screen. O2 drives off of the screen and O1 rolls facing the ball for a return pass.

Diagram #8: O1 dribbles the ball toward O2. If O2 is overplayed and cannot get a direct pass, he reverses direction and goes to the basket for a back door pass from O1.

Diagram #9: O1 dribbles the ball toward O2. O2 comes up and sets a rear screen for O1. O1 dribbles off of the screen and O2 rolls facing the ball.

Diagram #10: O1 has the ball and passes it to O2. O1 follows his pass and receives an inside hand-off from O2.

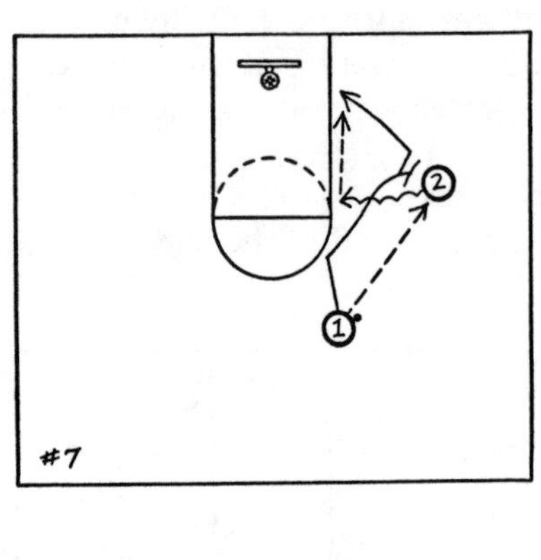

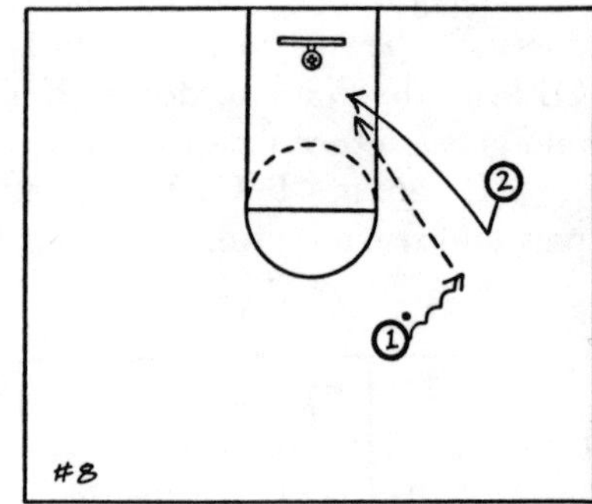

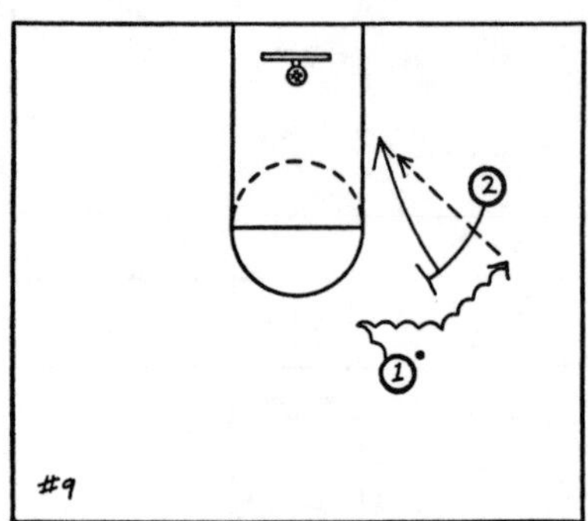

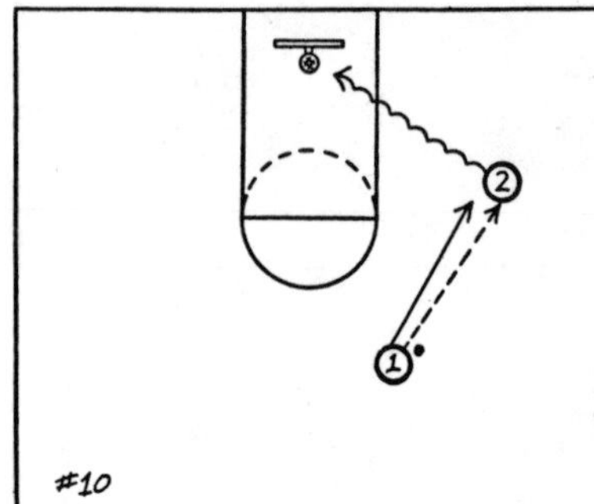

COACH DON SICKO—UNIVERSITY OF DETROIT

Coach Sicko has been coaching for seventeen years. Five of those seventeen have been at the college level. He has an overall won/lost record of 165 wins and 82 losses. His teams have won several city, league and district championships. He was named Michigan High School Coach of the Year in 1978.

PIVOT OUT OF TROUBLE

Purpose: To teach players the proper footwork when they have used their dribble and they are being pressured
Personnel and Equipment Needed: A coach or manager, a minimum of six players, three basketballs and the entire floor
Teaching Points: 1) Keep knees bent. 2) Use a small radius pivot. 3) Keep the ball low. 4) Keep the ball away from the defender.

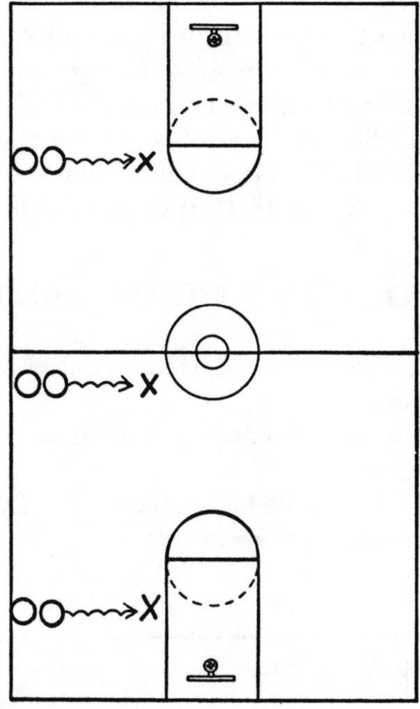

Directions: Have your players line up in three lines as diagrammed. The first player in each line comes out about ten feet and becomes the defense. The next player in each line has a ball, they dribble out to the defender, and pick up their dribble on purpose. The offense then makes a reverse pivot away from the defender who does everything he can to harass the offensive player. The defender can even foul the offensive player somewhat. This gets the offensive player ready for the no-call slaps. The defensive player should be as aggressive and heady as possible. Example—faking one way and coming back the other. He should attack the ball. The offensive player stays low to the floor with his knees and keeps his pivot foot stationary. The foot he can move should be with a short step so his radius is small. The coach or manager blows the whistle after six or seven seconds and they rotate. The offensive player becomes the new defensive player and the defensive player goes to the end of the line.

COACH DOUG HINES—MISSISSIPPI COLLEGE

Coach Hines has been in coaching for thirty years. Twenty-two of those thirty have been at the collegiate level. He has a won/lost record of 130 wins and 113 losses at Mississippi College and 236 wins and 168 losses overall. His teams have been nationally ranked on numerous occasions. He has been honored as Gulf South Athletic Conference Coach of the Year in 1977 and 1978. He was also honored as National Coach of the Year for NCAA Division II, District III in 1978.

TRIANGLE TIPPING DRILL

Purpose: To improve timing, fingertab control of the ball, jumping ability and conditioning.
Personnel and Equipment Needed: A minimum of three players, one basketball and a basket
Teaching Points: 1) Tip the ball at the height of your jump. 2) Make a controlled tip (two hands if necessary).

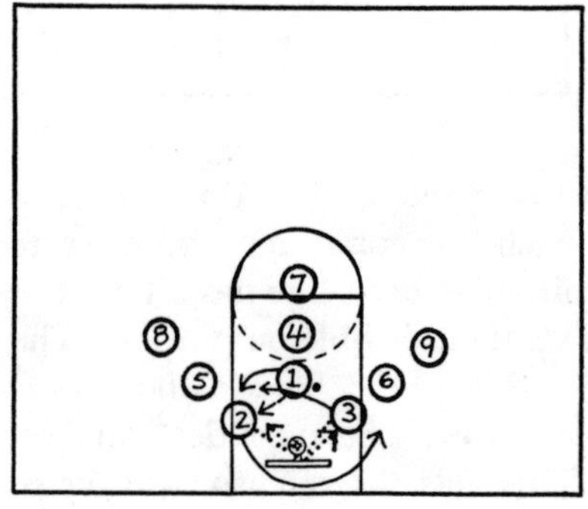

Directions: Divide the players into three lines as shown. O1 tosses the ball over the head of O2 and cuts behind him. O2 makes a controlled tip high over the basket against the board to O3 and cuts under the basket and goes behind O3. The O3 tips the ball to O1 and goes behind O1. O1 tips the ball to O2 and the drill continues. Have the players successfully make 20 tips in a row before they are finished. When they finish, they go to the end of the line and three more (O4, O5 and O6) come out.

Part VI

REBOUNDING DRILLS

COACH BUD HARBIN—MT. VERNON NAZARENE COLLEGE

Coach Harbin has been coaching for sixteen years. Eight of those sixteen have been at the college level. He has an overall won/lost record of 196 wins and 189 losses.

MASS BOX-OUT DRILL

Purpose: To teach boxing-out techniques
Personnel and Equipment Needed: One coach, entire team of players and the entire floor
Teaching Points: 1) Reverse-pivot on box-out. 2) Make contact with your offensive player. 3) Stay low with a wide base for stability.

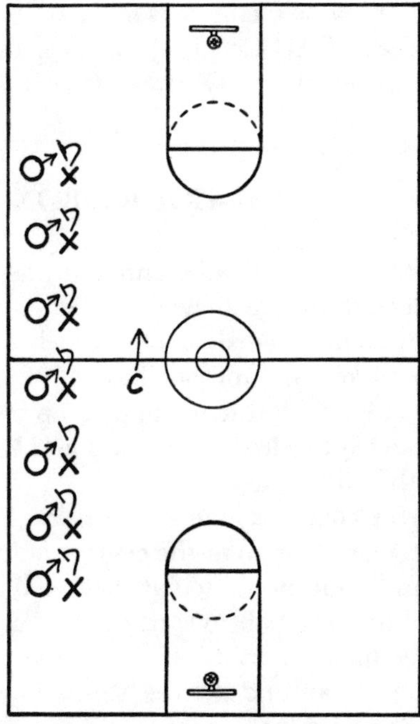

Directions: Divide the team into two groups. One group is on offense and the other group is on defense. Have them spread out across the court as diagrammed. The coach stands behind the defense. When the coach holds out his hand to the right this keys the offensive players to move in that direction. Make sure the offense makes a penetrating move toward the coach. The defense uses a reverse pivot to box them out. If the coach holds out his left hand, the offense moves in that direction and the defense makes contact again with a reverse pivot. After several times, have the offense and defense change places. This is a good drill to teach boxing-out principles and techniques. It is used primarily as a lead-up drill to other more advanced drills.

COACH JAMES CALHOUN—NORTHEASTERN UNIVERSITY

Coach Calhoun has been coaching for eighteen years. Fourteen of those eighteen have been at the college level. He has a won/lost record at Northeastern University of 195 wins and 119 losses. His teams won the ECAC tournament in 1980–81 and 1981–82. His teams have also been the ECAC regular season champions in 1980, 1981, 1982 and 1984. He has been selected as ECAC Coach of the Year in 1973, 1980, 1982 and 1984. He has also been chosen District 1 Coach of the Year in 1973 and 1982.

ONE-ON-ONE HALF-COURT BOX DRILL

Purpose: To improve box-out skills and attitudes, reactions to the ball and ability to defend the break-away.
Personnel and Equipment Needed: One coach or manager, entire team of players, two basketballs and one basket
Teaching Points: 1) Force the offense to pick-up his dribble. 2) Make contact on the box-out. 3) Secure the rebound and keep the ball above your head. 4) Snap the outlet pass.
Directions: Have the coach or manager position himself at the hash mark. Then have the team line up at the center circle. Have one defensive man come out and position himself at the free throw line. The drill begins with O1 dribbling the ball toward the basket. Once he reaches the free throw line, he has two dribbles in which to do something. The defender (X) picks up O1 around the free throw line or above and attempts to force O1 to pull up for a jump shot. Once the shot is taken, X must box-out O1 and secure the rebound. As soon as the ball is rebounded and outletted to the coach or manager, X must react to the

next offensive player (O2) who is already on the way. The defense stays for a certain number consecutively, usually a percentage of the team. Then a new defensive player comes out and the drill continues.

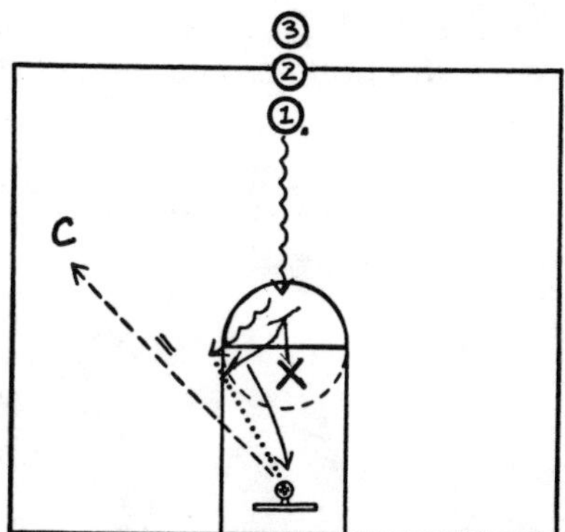

COACH GEORGE RAVELING—UNIVERSITY OF IOWA

Coach Raveling has been coaching for twenty-two years all at the collegiate level. He has an overall won/lost record of 167 wins and 136 losses. Coach Raveling was selected as the assistant coach for the 1984 USA Olympic Team. He was the head coach for the U.S.A. Select Team in 1982. He was also the PAC-8 Conference and UPI West Coast Coach of the Year in 1975.

WORKHORSE DRILL

Purpose: To improve rebounding techniques
Personnel and Equipment Needed: One coach, an entire team of players, one basketball and a basket
Teaching Points: 1) Take a good jump shot. 2) Follow your shot. 3) Stay low and wide on your reverse pivot. 4) Box-out aggressively.
Directions: Divide the team into two lines as shown above. The "O" line is the "workhorse" line and the "X" line is the one-on-one line. The drill starts with O1 sprinting to a position about five feet from the base-

line. He comes to a jump stop and reverse-pivots. After pivoting he receives a pass from the coach. He squares up to the basket and takes a jump shot. The ball is rebounded by the shooter and outletted to X1. O1 then quickly advances out to meet X1 and will now play him one-on-one. X1 can have only three dribbles with the ball. Stress blocking out by O1 once the shot has been taken by X1. X1 and O1 switch lines and the drill continues. Work this drill on both sides of the floor.

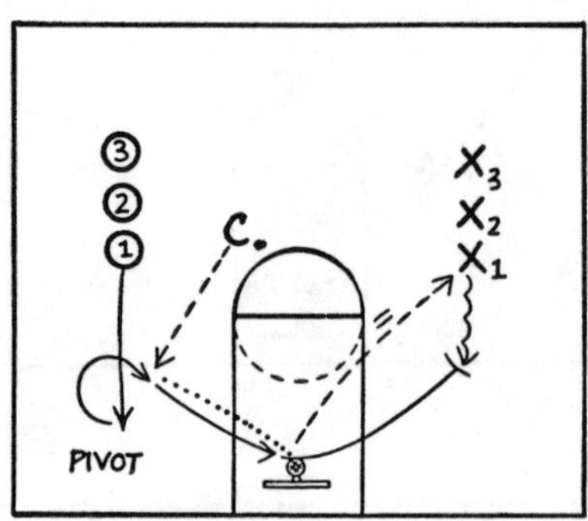

COACH DICK DAMRON—KENTUCKY CHRISTIAN COLLEGE

Coach Damron has been coaching for six years all at the college level. In those six years he has compiled a won/lost record of 116 wins and 62 losses. His team finished third in the nation in the National Christian College Athletic Association Division II in 1979 and fourth in the nation in 1978 and 1980. He was named National Christian College Athletic Association Division II Coach of the Year in 1980.

TWO-MAN REBOUNDING DRILL

Purpose: To teach the proper method of boxing-out and making an outlet pass

Personnel and Equipment Needed: An entire team of players, one basketball and the entire floor

Teaching Points: 1) Make contact and then release to the ball. 2) Execute a two-handed overhead pass to the wing. 3) Make a quick transition into offense.

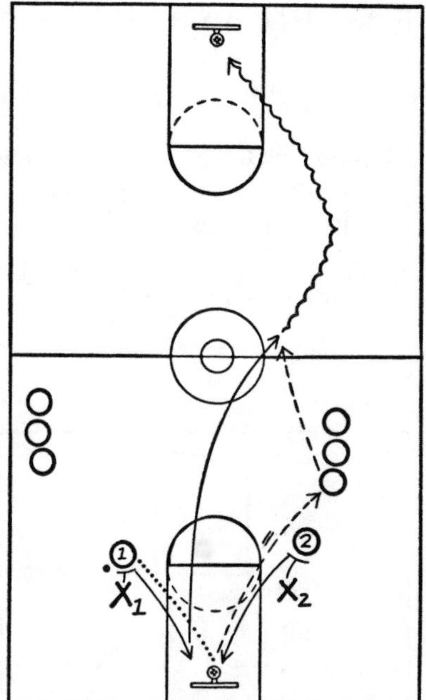

Directions: Divide the team into pairs, one pair on offense, one pair on defense, with the other pairs lined up at the hash marks. The pair on offense (O1 and O2) have the ball and put up a shot under pressure. The defensive pair (X1 and X2) must box O1 and O2 out and go for the rebound. Once rebounded, the ball is outletted to a player standing at the hash marks. The defensive player who did not get the rebound sprints to the other end and receives a pass from the player to whom the outlet was made. Upon receiving the ball, he takes it in for a lay-up. O1 and O2 become defense, a new pair from the hash marks becomes offense and X1 and X2 go to the hash marks. Anytime the defense yields a rebound to the offense, that pair must run five sprints.

COACH BENJAMIN BRAUN—SIENA HEIGHTS COLLEGE

Coach Braun has been in coaching for seven years. Five of those seven have been at the collegiate level. At Siena Heights he has compiled a won/lost record of 100 wins and 64 losses. Coach Braun was named NAIA District 23 Coach of the Year in 1982.

BOX-OUT AND GO DRILL

Purpose: To improve the fundamentals of boxing-out and outletting the ball
Personnel and Equipment Needed: Two coaches, a minimum of seven players, one basketball and the entire floor
Teaching Points: 1) Box-out properly. 2) Make a good outlet pass (half turn to the outside). 3) Outlets come to meet your pass. 4) On the two-on-one fast break, emphasize the conversion of a lay-up, not a jump shot.

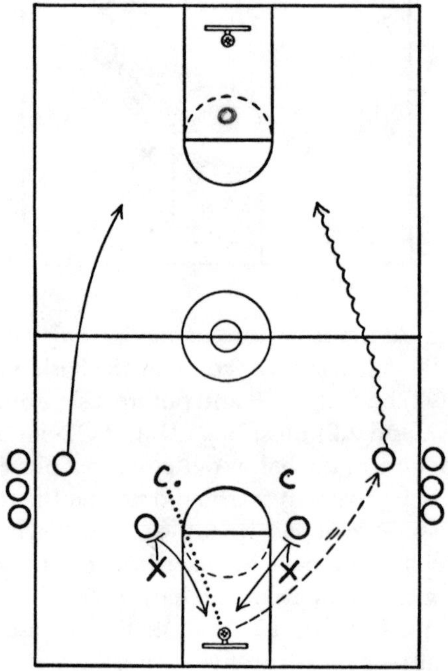

Directions: Position the two coaches in the guard positions as shown. They can pass the ball to the offense or shoot it themselves. Bring two players out on offense, two players out on defense and two players out as outlets. One player goes to the other end to play defense. The rest of the squad lines up on the sideline at the free throw line extended. When a shot goes up, the defense must box-out their man and secure the rebound. Then they outlet the ball to the near side outlet man. The outlets take the ball two-on-one to the other end to convert a lay-up. If they fail to make the lay-up, they run a lap. The players rotate as follows: The next player in each line becomes the offense, the offense becomes the defense, the defense becomes the outlet and one of the outlet men stays as defense at the other end. The other outlet man and former defensive man go to the end of the lines.

COACH DON MANESS—BARTLESVILLE WESLEYAN COLLEGE

Coach Maness has been coaching for fourteen years at the college level. He has a won/lost record of 68 wins and 109 losses at Bartlesville Wesleyan and 138 wins and 156 losses overall.

EAGLE REBOUNDING DRILL

Purpose: To teach defensive and offensive rebounding techniques
Personnel and Equipment Needed: One coach, an entire team of players, one basketball and a basket
Teaching Points: 1) Correct pivot. 2) Body contact. 3) Release to the ball. 4) Wide base for stability. 5) Outside pivot for outlet pass.
Directions: Have six players come out on the floor, three on offense (O1, O2 and O3) and three on defense (X1, X2 and X3), as shown. The rest of the players divide up evenly and go to the hash marks. The coach positions himself as diagrammed, with the ball. The coach begins the drill by shooting the ball and the defense boxes-out the offense. After the rebound is secured, the defense outlets the ball to the players at the hash marks. If the offense rebounds the ball, play continues as in a game situation, three-on-three, until another shot is taken. You do not rotate until there is a defensive rebound. The rotation is as follows: O4 replaces O1, O1 replaces X1, X1 becomes O2, O2 becomes X2, X2 replaces O3, O3 replaces X3 and X3 rotates out to the hash mark behind O8 and O7 moves across the floor to the other hash mark behind O6. See end "B" for the rotation.

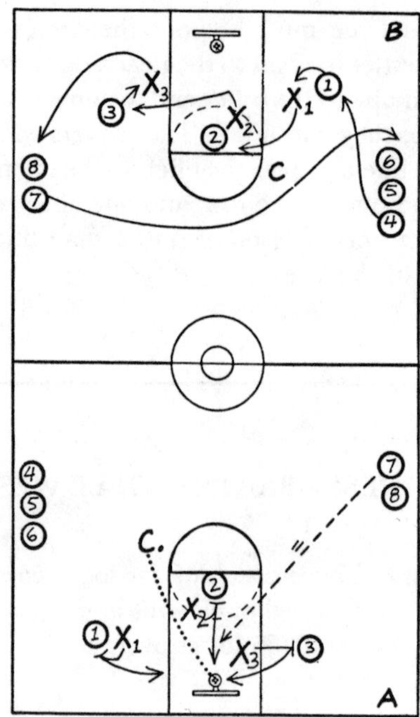

COACH RICHARD WHITMORE—COLBY COLLEGE

Coach Whitmore has been coaching for nineteen years. Fourteen of those nineteen have been at the college level. He has achieved an overall won/lost record of 263 wins and 154 losses. At Colby College he has won 183 and lost 118. His teams won the MIAA championship in 1972 and 1974. He was named the Maine College Coach of the Year in 1973, 1975, 1981. He was also selected as the Northeast and New England College Coach of the Year, Division III in 1982 and 1983.

REBOUNDING COMBINATION DRILL

Purpose: To improve rebounding skills for both the offense and the defense

Personnel and Equipment Needed: Two coaches and/or managers, minimum of six players, one basketball and a basket

Teaching Points: 1) Contact and pivot angles on the box-out. 2) Reactions to situations in motion offense or defense. 3) Understanding of the task—box-out then get the ball. 4) Offensive rebounding techniques and routes. 5) "Shot" called out by all defensive players when the ball is released.

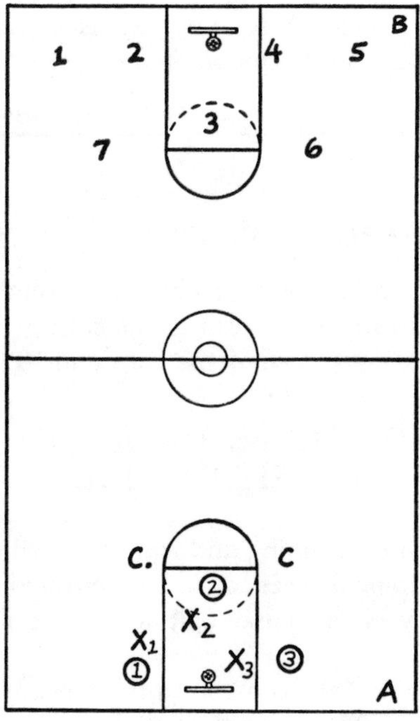

Directions: Have three offensive players position themselves in any of the seven spots shown in the diagram above at end "B." The defense then assumes its positions in relation to their men and the ball. The coaches position themselves at the elbows and one of them has the ball. The coach decides the emphasis of the day; offensive, defensive inside, help side, zone, etc. The ball is shot and the offensive men head to the basket and the defensive men box them out.

The progression is basically as follows:

1) Stationary inside positions.
2) Stationary outside positions.
3) Movement by the offense—defensive concentration.
4) Movement by the defense—defensive concentration.

5) Movement by the offense—offensive concentration.
6) Movement by the defense—offensive concentration.

Variations:

1) Pass the ball to the other coach or manager and adjust defensive positions.
2) Call out "move" and have the offense and the defense move one position clockwise or counter clockwise.
3) The ball is always shot while movement is taking place.

COACH BRUCE HAROLDSON—MONTANA STATE

Coach Haroldson has been coaching for twenty-three years. Sixteen of those twenty-three have been at the college level. He has compiled an overall won/lost record of 152 wins and 101 losses.

THREE-ON-THREE REBOUNDING AND TRANSITION DRILL

Purpose: To teach rebounding and transition skills
Personnel and Equipment Needed: Two coaches and/or managers, minimum of six players, one basketball, a rebound ring and the entire floor
Teaching Points: 1) Make contact on the box-out. 2) Make a sharp pass to the outlet man. 3) Work on the transition from offense to defense and vice versa.
Directions: Three offensive players (O1, O2, and O3) position themselves on the court as diagrammed. Then, three defensive players (X1, X2, and X3) assume their positions in relation to their men and the ball. The coach has the ball and he instructs the offense to "move around" the basket area. On the coach's shot, the defense will box-out and go for the rebound. If the defense gets the rebound, they outlet the ball to one of the coaches who takes the ball on the dribble to the other end. The offensive team must hustle back on defense and stop his penetration. At this point, the defensive team drops off and the offensive team becomes defense, and a new offensive team (O4, O5, and O6) waiting under the basket comes out. If the offensive team gets the rebound, the defensive team must stay on defense and go again against another offensive (O4, O5, and O6) who are waiting under the basket. This gives the offensive rebounding team incentive.

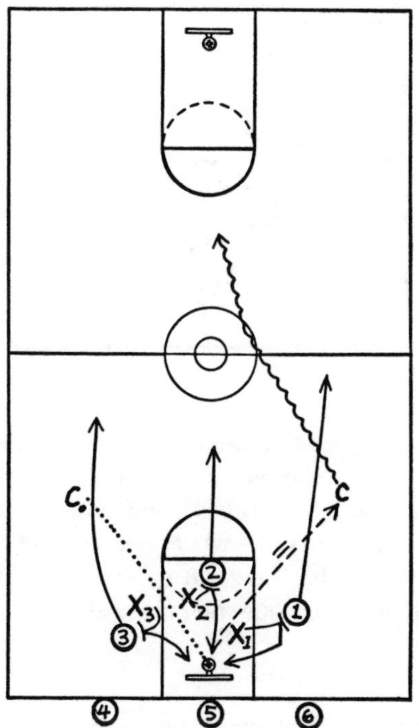

COACH MICHAEL L. GARMAN—MILLERSVILLE STATE COLLEGE

Coach Garman has been coaching for seven years. Three of those seven have been at the college level.

MARAUDER REBOUNDING DRILL

Purpose: To teach proper boxing-out skills
Personnel and Equipment Needed: One coach or manager, a minimum of six players, one basketball and a basket.
Teaching Points: 1) Be aggressive on the box-out. 2) Talk on defense. 3) React quickly to find your man.
Directions: X1 and X2 are on defense and will be doing the boxing-out. O1, O2, O3 and O4 will position themselves along the free throw lane as diagrammed. The coach has the ball and he calls out two numbers: one and three and then shoots the ball. The defense must communicate and box-out the offensive players who have been called out and

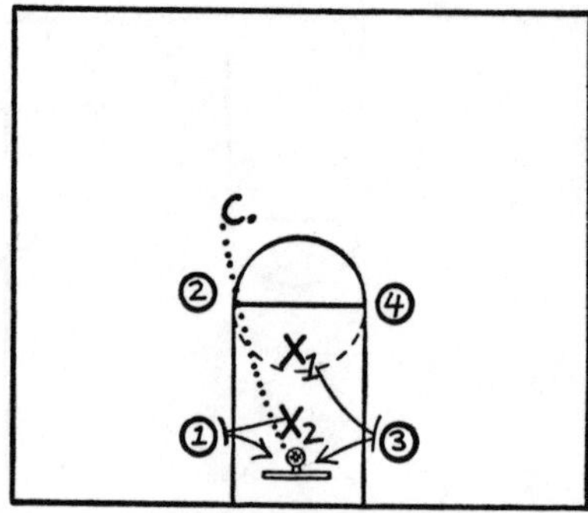

rebound the ball. Only the two offensive players who have been called out can go for the offensive rebound. The defense goes three times and then they rotate and take O1 and O2 positions on offense and O1 and O2 become O3 and O4, and O3 and O4 become the defense. The drill is continued until everyone has been on defense.

Variation: You can call out the offensive players' names instead of their numbers.

COACH CURT TONG—WILLIAMS COLLEGE

Coach Tong has been coaching at the collegiate level for eighteen years. He has compiled a won/lost record of 100 wins and 93 losses at Williams College and 238 wins and 146 losses overall. His teams have won the Little Three Conference championship three times and also the Ohio Athletic Conference championship (Southern Division) three times. He was named the Ohio Athletic Conference Coach of the Year in 1971.

BOX-OUT DRILL

Purpose: To teach boxing-out techniques and ball protection
Personnel and Equipment Needed: One coach or manager, ten players, one basketball and the entire floor
Teaching Points: 1) Box-out properly. 2) Protect the ball by keeping it high and pivoting away from traffic. 3) Make a good outlet pass to start the fast break.

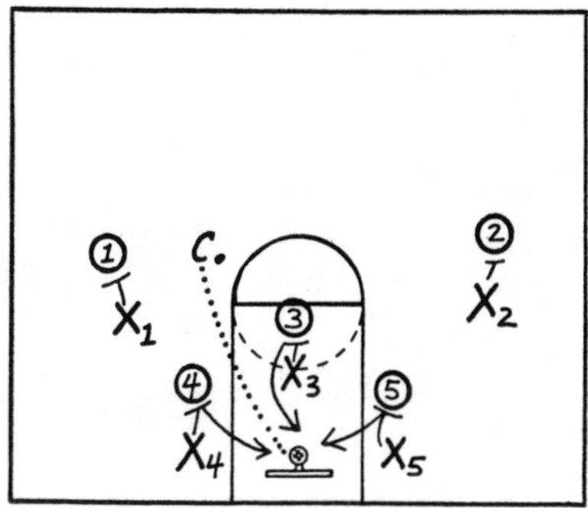

Directions: Divide the players into two teams. One is on offense (O1–05) and one is on defense (X1–X5). Players X3, X4, and X5 take their defensive positions in relation to their men and the ball, which is with the coach. When the ball is shot, X3, X4 and X5 box-out their offensive opponents. Players X1 and X2 also box-out but are not involved in the rebounding aspect of this drill. As soon as either X3, X4 or X5 rebounds the ball, they protect it against immediate transitional pressure by squeezing it and pivoting away from trouble. At the same time, they are looking to outlet the ball to X1 or X2. X1 and X2 must get themselves open to receive the outlet pass. When they receive the outlet pass, the fast break commences for X1, X2, X3, X4 and X5. O1, O2, O3, O4 and O5 must make the transition to defense by locating the ball and assuming the desired defensive positions.

Part VII

SHOOTING DRILLS

COACH GEORGE FISHER—UNIVERSITY OF MINNESOTA—DULUTH

Coach Fisher has been coaching for ten years. Eight of those ten years have been at the college level. He has a won/lost record of 131 wins and 83 losses for a .612 winning percentage. His teams were NAIA District 13 champions in 1981 and Northern Intercollegiate Conference champions in 1982. He was selected NAIA District 12 Coach of the Year in 1978 and Wisconsin Independent Coaches Association Coach of the Year in 1978. He was also selected NIC Coach of the Year in 1982.

"POSSESSION CONTROL" FREE THROW SHOOTING DRILL

Purpose: To improve free throw shooting and possession control
Personnel and Equipment Needed: Ten players, one basketball and a basket
Teaching Points: 1) Free throw shooting concentration and technique. 2) Defensive and offensive rebounding.

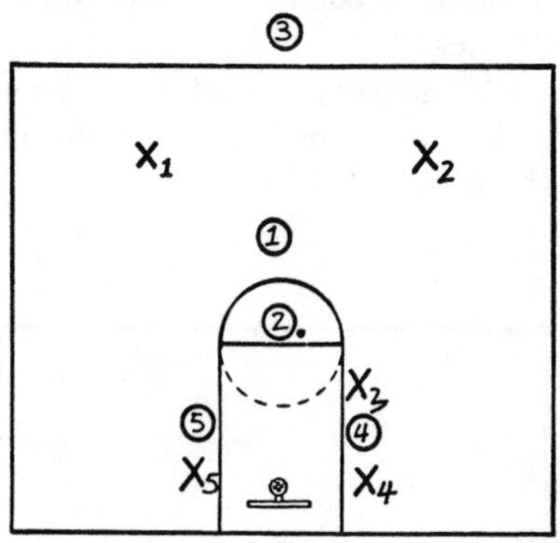

Directions: Divide the players into two teams. Each player on the offensive team shoots one free throw. The defensive team works on good block-out position and fast break initiation on a missed free throw. The other members of the offensive team look to tap back the missed free throw for possession control. When the offensive team makes eight out of ten attempts, they switch with the defensive team.

COACH NORM WILHELMI—THE KING'S COLLEGE—RETIRED

Coach Wilhelmi coached for twenty-eight years. Twenty-five were at the King's College. He compiled a won/lost record of 255–245 at the King's College and 283–273 overall. His teams won several tournament and conference championships. He was selected Seaboard Conference Coach of the Year and Mid-Atlantic Conference Coach of the Year. Coach Wilhelmi is also the Founding Father of the National Christian College Athletic Association.

COMPETITIVE FREE THROW DRILL

Purpose: To put pressure and fun into free throws and help develop fingertip tap control

Personnel and Equipment Needed: A minimum of four players, one basketball and one basket

Teaching Points: 1) Concentrate on the free throw. 2) Time jump so that you are tapping the ball at the height of your jump. 3) Tap the ball only, do not catch the ball.

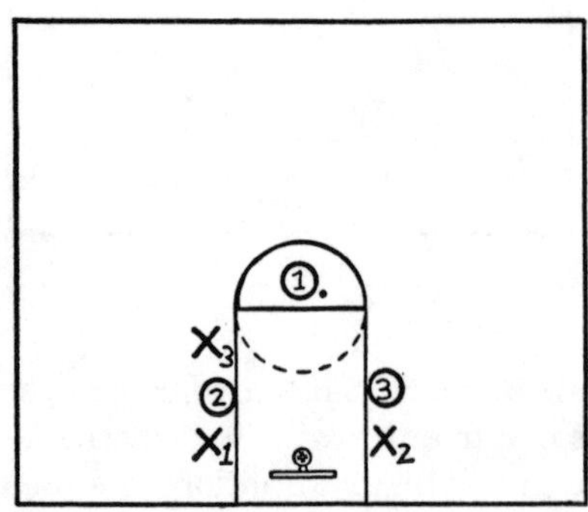

Directions: Divide your players into two teams. Have them line up on the free throw lane as they would in a game situation with one person as a shooter at the free throw line. Each shooter gets three free throws. If the shooters make all three they rotate clockwise. If they miss, the players lined up on the lane try to tap the ball in. They cannot catch the ball or shoot one-hand shots. They can tap-pass to a teammate, but if the ball is caught or touches the floor a violation occurs. After a violation, the shooter finishes his three attempts or they rotate. The game is to 21 points with one point for a made free throw and two points for a made tap. The game has to be won by a made free throw, not on a tap in.

Variation: On a missed free throw, regular play occurs. The offensive team tries to tap the ball in or rebound it and the defensive team tries to rebound the ball. After the ball is rebounded, that team moves the ball out past the free throw line and goes into their regular half-court offense, and the other team goes on defense. They go until the offense scores or turns the ball over. Then the free throw shooter continues his attempts or they rotate clockwise. The game is to 21 points, with one point for a free throw and two points for a field goal.

DR. GENE MEHAFFEY—OHIO WESLEYAN UNIVERSITY

Coach Mehaffey has been coaching for twenty-five years. Twenty of those twenty-five years have been at the college level. He has a won/lost record of 371 wins and 196 losses. His teams won the Volunteer State Athletic Conference championship in 1969, 1972, and 1973. He was selected NAIA District 24 Coach of the Year in 1970, 1972, and 1973, and NAIA Area V Coach of the Year in 1970.

FREE THROWS "PRESSURE'S ON" DRILL

Purpose: To shoot free throws in a competitive situation
Personnel and Equipment Needed: Four to fifteen players, two basketballs and two baskets
Teaching Points: 1) Concentrate on shooting the free throw, using your regular routine.

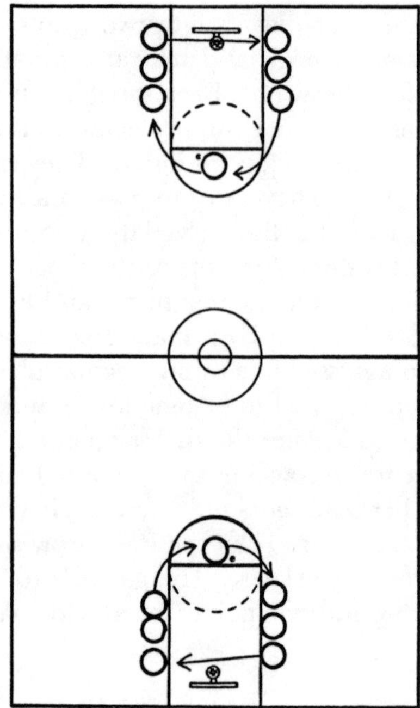

Directions: One player goes to the free throw line to shoot one free throw. If the player makes the free throw, he doesn't run the designated penalty (a sprint). If he misses the free throw, he has one penalty to run if the next shooter makes his free throw. If the second shooter misses, the penalty is doubled. This is continued by doubling the penalty on successive misses until a shot is made. The drill consists of a predetermined number of rounds. However, if the last shooter doesn't make the shot, the players continue shooting until a shot is made to end the round.

COACH THOMAS MARSHALL, ASSISTANT COACH—UNIVERSITY OF CALIFORNIA, SAN DIEGO

Coach Marshall has been coaching for five years. Two of those years have been at the college level as an assistant coach. He has compiled a won/lost overall record of 46 wins and 34 losses.

FREE THROW LINE DRILL

Purpose: To simulate fourth-quarter fatigue while shooting free throws

Personnel and Equipment Needed: Entire team, coach, one basketball and a basket

Teaching Points: 1) Proper free throw form and concentration. 2) Disregarding fatigue while focusing full attention on proper completion of drill.

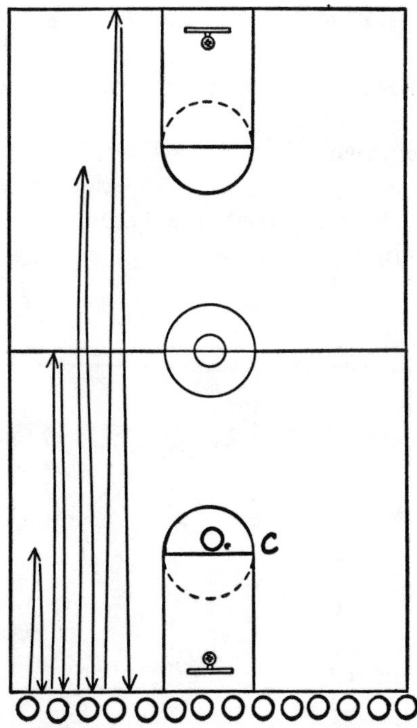

Directions: Players (at the end of a practice session) line up across the baseline. The coach picks one player to shoot ten free throws without missing. If a shot is missed, all players run one line drill (suicide). The coach now picks another player to shoot nine free throws. Again if he misses, all players run a suicide. Should all the free throws be made the drill ends. The coach should work his way down to one free throw, and if this is missed, continue up to ten again.

COACH JIM O'BRIEN—WHEELING COLLEGE

Coach O'Brien has been coaching for nine years all at the college level. He finished his first year as a head coach with a won/lost record of 17 wins and 14 losses. He was named NAIA District 28 Coach of the Year and West Virginia Intercollegiate Athletic Conference Coach of the Year in 1983.

MULTIPURPOSE TWO LINE LAY-UP DRILL

Purpose: To develop skills in passing, sprinting, catching, pivoting and shooting near the basket
Personnel and Equipment Needed: A minimum of six players, two basketballs and a basket
Teaching Points: 1) Make hard, quick passes. 2) Stay low on the reverse pivot. 3) Use the board on the lay-up.

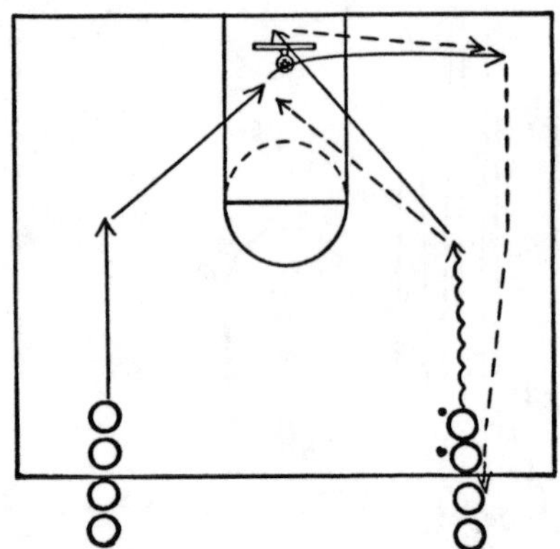

Directions: Have your players form two lines at half-court. The first two players in the right-hand line have balls. The drill begins by having the first player in the right-hand line dribble the ball to the free throw line extended where he comes to a jump stop and executes a reverse pivot. He then makes a chest pass to the first player in the left hand line, who has sprinted to the free throw line extended and is coming at a 45 degree angle to the basket. The pass is hard and to the target that the receiver is giving. The lay-up is off the backboard. The passer rebounds and passes the ball to the shooter in the corner, who in turn passes to the next player in the right-hand line without a ball. Perform the following shots in this order: 1) lay-ups on the left side; 2) right-hand hook after sprinting through the middle. 3) jump stop, pump fake and power lay-up left side; 4) change lines and do the same shots from the other side. The first two players, upon completing the drill, go to the end of the opposite line.

COACH DON HARNUM—SUSQUEHANNA UNIVERSITY

Coach Harnum has been coaching for twelve years at the college level. He has compiled a won/lost record of 97 wins and 80 losses at Susquehanna University and 163 wins and 140 losses overall.

"RANGE FINDER" DRILL

Purpose: To develop shooting technique and touch
Personnel and Equipment Needed: Two players, one basketball and a basket
Teaching Points: 1) Shooting hand behind the ball. 2) Eyes fixed on a specific target. 3) Ball rolled on release above the eyes. 4) Follow through with the two shooting fingers in the basket.

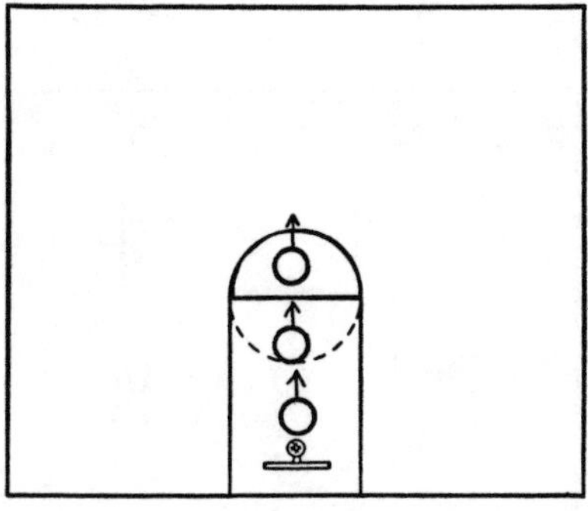

Directions: The shooter starts three feet from the basket and makes three in a row with emphasis on perfect technique and concentration. His partner is coaching him on the four teaching points. After making three in a row, the shooter steps back a step to make three more in a row. This procedure continues until you no longer can use the perfect technique because you are too far from the basket. Now you have found your "standing range." The jump shot range is one step deeper than the standing range.

COACH LEE H. ROSE—UNIVERSITY OF SOUTH FLORIDA

Coach Rose has been coaching for fifteen years at the college level. He has a won/lost record of 317–114 for an impressive .735 winning percentage. His teams won the Sun Belt Conference in 1976–77, 1977–78, the NCAA Mideast Regional in 1977 and 1980, the Big Ten Conference in 1978–79, and the Florida Four tournament in 1982. He was selected Sun Belt Conference Coach of the Year in 1977, Sporting News National Coach of the Year in 1977, UPI's Big Ten Conference Co-Coach of the Year in 1980.

JUMP SHOT DRILL

Purpose: Teach twelve-to fifteen-foot bank shots
Personnel and Equipment Needed: Six to fifteen players, two basketballs and a basket
Teaching Points: 1) Catch the ball with knees bent. 2) Pivot on inside foot and square up to the basket. 3) Concentrate on spot on backboard.

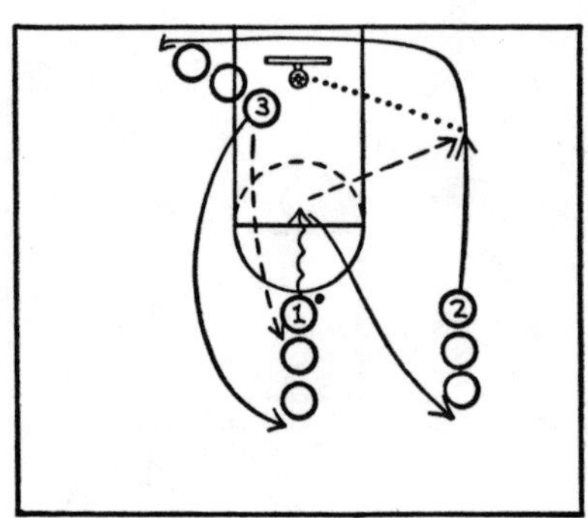

Directions: Have players form three lines: line one at the top of the key; line two at the top of the key extended out to the wing (either right or left side); and line three under the basket. The first two players in line one have the balls. The first player in line one dribbles to the free throw line and passes the ball to the first player in line two who has moved to within twelve-to fifteen-foot range on the side. Player in line two receives the pass and shoots a bank shot. The first player in line three rebounds the shot. After the shot, the next player in each line continues the drill. The first players rotate to the following lines; passer (line 1) becomes shooter (line 2), shooter (line 2) becomes rebounder (line 3), and rebounder (line 3) becomes passer (line 1).

COACH MICHAEL E. LONG—COLLEGE OF SAINT ROSE

Coach Long has been coaching at the college level for eleven years. He has compiled a won/lost record of 129 wins and 120 losses at the College of Saint Rose and 139 wins and 130 losses overall. His teams won the Northeastern Athletic Conference in 1977–78, 1978–79, 1979–80, and 1980–81.

COMPETITIVE SPOT-SHOOTING DRILL

Purpose: To improve jump shooting
Personnel and Equipment Needed: Minimum of six players, four basketballs and two baskets
Teaching Points: 1) Quick release. 2) Shot concentration. 3) Follow through. 4) Keep feet moving and have hands always ready to receive the pass.

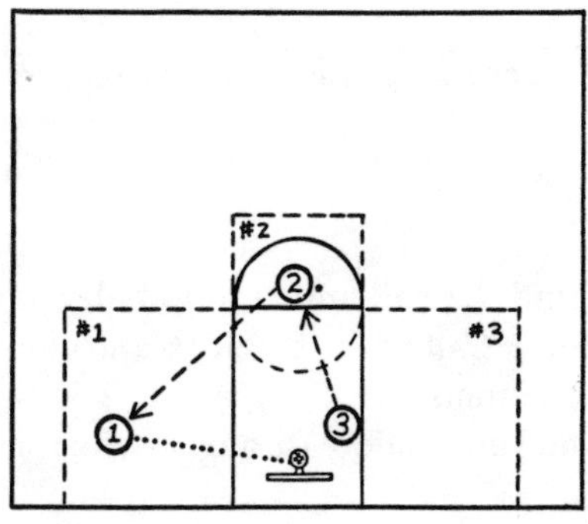

Directions: Number 1 is the shooter, number 2 is the passer and number 3 is the rebounder. Numbers 2 and 3 start with the basketballs. On the whistle, number 2 passes his ball to number 1 and number 3 passes his ball to number 2. Number 1 shoots the basketball and looks to number 2 for the next pass. Number 3 rebounds the shot and passes the ball to number 2. This is repeated until number 1 has made ten shots from area number 1. Number 2 then becomes the shooter, number 3 the passer, and number 1 the rebounder. Once all three players have made ten shots in area number 1, they move to shooting area number 2 and repeat the process, and then they finish the drill in area number 3. The first group to finish the drill wins. The other teams continue to shoot until they finish. The first teams to finish shoot one and ones while they wait for the rest to finish. The losing teams run a suicide.

COACH HAL WISSEL—UNIVERSITY OF NORTH CAROLINA AT CHARLOTTE

Coach Wissel has been coaching for eighteen years at the college level at five different institutions. He has compiled a won/lost record of 261 wins and 233 losses. His teams have won several tournament championships, including the NCAA Division II national championship in 1981. He was named Sunshine State Conference Coach of the Year in 1979, 1980, and 1982. He also received one of the profession's highest honors in 1980, when the NABC named him Division II National Coach of the Year.

THREE-MAN QUICK SHOOTING DRILL

Purpose: To catch the ball in position and shoot with quickness and balance in one motion
Personnel and Equipment Needed: Three players and two basketballs for each basket
Teaching Points:

Shooting:

1. Jump behind the ball and land in balance facing the basket, and catch the ball with the block-and-tuck method.
2. Shoot in one motion.
3. Exaggerate your follow-through before moving on to the next spot.

Rebounding:

1. Be in position to rebound with a good stance on the balls of your feet, with both hands up.
2. Jump and rebound the ball with both hands.
3. Land in balance keeping the ball above your forehead.
4. Fake and make a good two-hand overhead outlet pass.

Passing:

1. Be in a triple-threat stance with weight on your pivot foot and eyes looking at the basket.
2. See the receiver without looking at him.
3. Aim for the shooter's shooting hand.
4. Make all passes with two hands, using either chest or overhead passes.

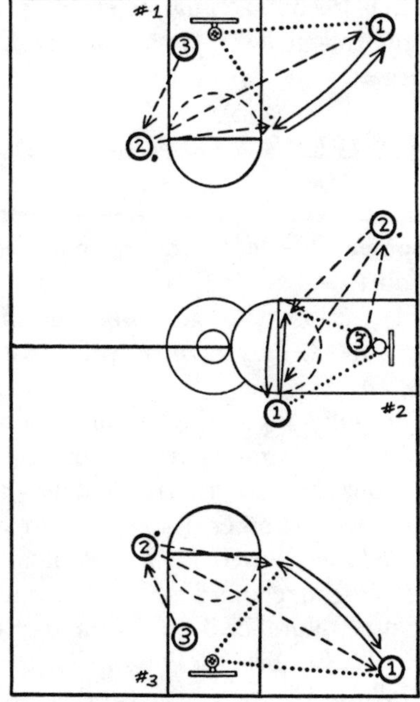

Directions: Number 1 is the shooter, he starts with a ball and shoots the ball first in the right corner spot. He then moves to the right elbow to receive the next ball, catching the ball in position to shoot facing the basket. He continues moving back and forth from corner to elbow for 55 seconds. Number 2 is the passer and he starts at the opposite elbow and passes the ball to the shooter's shooting hand when the shooter gives a target. Number 3 is the rebounder and he rebounds the shot with two hands and passes it to the passer with a two-hand overhead pass. After 55 seconds, the players rotate in five seconds, with number 1 (shooter) becoming number 3 (rebounder), number 3 (rebounder) becoming number 2 (passer) and number 2 (passer) becoming number 1 (shooter). After three minutes, they change to the next shooting area (right elbow to left elbow) and after another three minutes they advance to the third shooting area (left elbow to left corner). See the diagram for the three shooting areas. The drill takes nine minutes and each player should get at least 50 shots.

COACH CHUCK BOERGER—CONCORDIA COLLEGE

Coach Boerger has been coaching for eleven years. Two of those eleven have been at the college level. He has an overall won/lost record of 105 wins and 95 losses.

THREE JUMPERS AND A LAY-UP DRILL

Purpose: To improve shooting on the move—passing—conditioning
Personnel and Equipment Needed: Six or more players, one basketball and the entire court
Teaching Points: 1) Jump-stop to go straight up for jumper. 2) Outside lane players stay wide. 3) Players must sprint to eliminate the dribble.
Directions: Player number 2 gets the ball off the backboard and outlets it to either number 1 or number 3. If number 1 gets the ball, he passes to number 3 who is sprinting down the floor. Without dribbling, number 3 takes a jumper. Number 1 follows and gets the rebound. Meanwhile, number 2 has followed his outlet pass and is waiting at half-court. Number 1 gets the rebound and outlets it to number 3 who is cutting down the sideline. Number 3 passes the ball to number 2 who takes the second jumper. Number 3 follows in for the rebound. Meanwhile, number 1 has followed his outlet pass and is waiting at half-court. After number 2 takes his jumper, he releases down the floor to receive an outlet pass from number 3. Number 2 then passes to number 1 for the third jumper, and follows in to get the rebound. Number 2 outlets the ball to number 1 who has just shot and is sprinting down the sideline. Number 1 passes to number 3 who is breaking from half-court for a lay-up.

After the first group has shot three jumpers and a lay-up, the next group steps out and continues the drill. The drill goes for five minutes. Give two points for a jumper and one point for the lay-up. Set a goal in terms of total points for the drill. If it is not reached run a sprint or suicide.

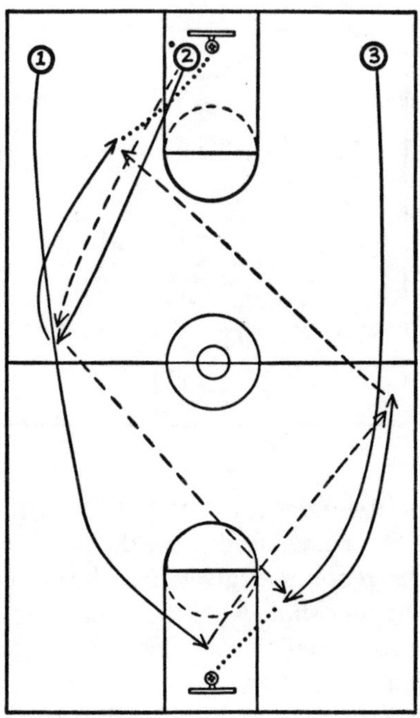

COACH RON RAINEY—UNIVERSITY OF DELAWARE

Coach Rainey has been coaching for twenty years. Seventeen of those twenty have been at the college level as either an assistant or a head coach. His teams at Chester High School achieved a won/lost record of 52 wins and only 17 losses in the three years he was there. In four seasons at Wilkes College, his teams won 52 games and lost 38. As an assistant at the University of Delaware he posted an overall won/lost record of 61 wins and 31 losses.

"MACHINE GUN" DRILL

Purpose: Quick release—shooting—conditioning
Personnel and Equipment Needed: Three players and two basketballs at each basket
Teaching Points: 1) Good rebound. 2) Good pass. 3) Quick release. 4) Be square to the basket. 5) Head up and eyes on the rim.

R — Rebounder

P — Passer

S — Shooter

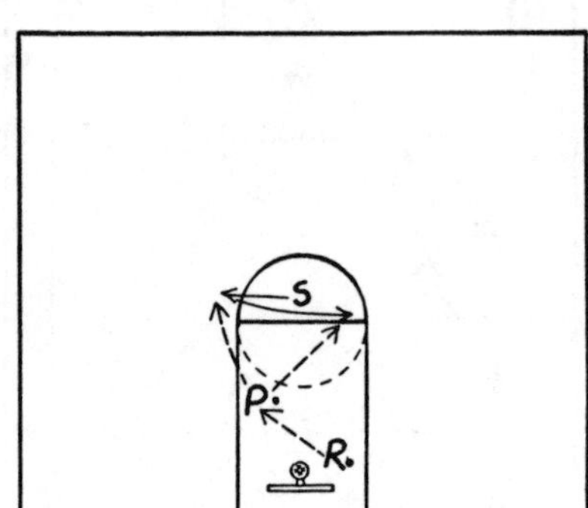

Directions: The rebounder and passer start with the two balls. The shooter moves and the passer feeds him the ball. As soon as the passer releases the ball, the rebounder gives him the second ball and he prepares to rebound the first shot. As soon as the shooter releases the shot, he moves to a new spot and the passer gets him the second ball. The drill continues in this manner for one minute. In that amount of time you should get between 20 to 25 shots attempted. After one minute, the players rotate positions; passer becomes shooter, shooter becomes rebounder, rebounder becomes passer. In three minutes all three players get a chance to shoot, to pass and to rebound. If you wish, at the end of three minutes have all players rotate one basket and start the drill again.

COACH CHET KAMMERER—WESTMONT COLLEGE

Coach Kammerer has been coaching for eighteen years all at the college level. He has a won/lost record of 337 wins and 180 losses. His teams have won several tournament and conference championships, including the NAIA District 3 championship in 1978. He was elected NAIA District 3 Coach of the Year in 1978 and 1981.

FIVE-SPOT SHOOTING DRILL

Purpose: Game shooting—under pressure—get to know shooting range
Personnel and Equipment Needed: Three players and two balls at each basket
Teaching Points: 1) Move clockwise and shoot, then move counterclockwise and shoot. 2) Stop, pivot on inside foot, and square to the basket. 3) Catch the ball with your knees bent. 4) Work on quick release.

Directions: The first player shoots a stationary shot at the first spot then he moves to the second spot and shoots. He continues this until he reaches the fifth spot. At the fifth spot, he shoots two shots then he moves to the fourth spot to shoot one shot and continues this until he reaches the first spot again. He should shoot a total of ten shots. Have a manager record the number made. Players 2 and 3 rebound and pass the ball to the shooter. They rotate in after each round of ten shots. Put the players under the pressure of a time limit. The three players should be able to shoot five rounds each in about eight minutes. Shoot five rounds twice each day for a total of 100 shots. Look for at least 65 percent from a shooter without any defense. If he falls below 65 percent, he is out of his range and should move in.

COACH HAL SMITH—MALONE COLLEGE

Coach Smith has been coaching for sixteen years all at the college level. He has compiled a won/lost record of 178 wins and 143 losses. His teams won the National Christian College Athletic Association District I tournament in 1974 and 1975. In 1974 they also won the NCCAA East Regional title and finished third at the national tournament. He was selected NCCAA District Coach of the Year in 1974, 1977, and 1978.

"SHARP SHOOTERS" DRILL

Purpose: Shoot under pressure—rebound and outlet the ball quickly
Personnel and Equipment Needed: Two players and one basketball at each basket, stopwatch or scoreclock
Teaching Points: 1) Make sure you are square to the basket before shooting. 2) Bend knees before catching the ball. 3) Concentrate. 4) Follow through. 5) Rebound and outlet the ball quickly.

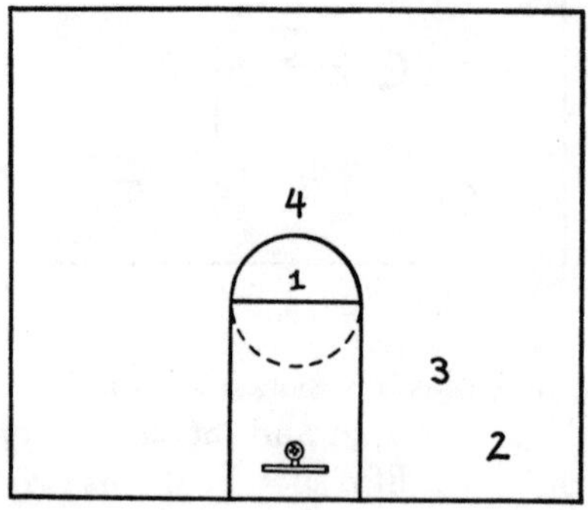

Directions: Two players make up a team, one shooting and one rebounding. Each player shoots for 30 seconds from the first of the four spots indicated on the diagram. At the end of 30 seconds, the coach calls out "switch" and the shooter and the rebounder switch positions. On the next switch, the original shooter goes to the next spot (#2) and shoots for 30 seconds. This continues until both players have shot at all four spots. Record each team's total points at the end of the drill. Keep a record of the highest total for the year. The drill should take about five minutes. The following are the types of shots and points for each spot:

Spot #1—Jump shot—one point
Spot #2—Jump shot—two points
Spot #3—Bank shot—two points
Spot #4—Set shot—three points

Have players vary the distances of the spots to stay within their shooting range.

Variations:

(1) Require the shooter to move to each spot one to four consecutively within the 30 seconds instead of staying at the same spot for the entire 30 seconds. Give each player four 30 second turns within the five minutes allotted for the drill.
(2) Require each team to score a minimum of 70 points or run a sprint.

COACH JIM KESSLER—GRACE COLLEGE

Coach Kessler has been coaching for twelve years. Six of those have been at the college level. He has a won/lost record of 116 wins and 82 losses. His teams won the Mid-Central Conference title in 1981–82 and 1982–83. He was selected M.C.C. Coach of the Year in 1982 and National Christian College Athletic Association District 3 Coach of the Year in 1980 and 1983. He also received N.C.C.A.A. Coach of the Year honors in 1983.

FOUR-MAN ROTATION SHOOTING DRILL

Purpose: To practice shooting with defense and rebounding with a specified pass

Personnel and Equipment Needed: Four players, one basketball and a basket

Teaching Points: 1) Practice shooting over defense. 2) Teach shooter to fill baseline, come to meet the pass, and square up. 3) Designate the type of pass to be used to stress concentration.

Directions: Player number 1 defends player number 2 with a hand in his face. After the shot, number 1 blocks out and releases for the rebound. Upon securing the rebound, number 1 passes the ball to number 4 who breaks out to the free throw line on the shot to become the feeder. Number 4 feeds the ball to number 3 who broke to the baseline from the free throw line on the shot. Number 2 turns and picks up number 3 and defends him with a hand in the face. This rotation continues for at least five minutes.

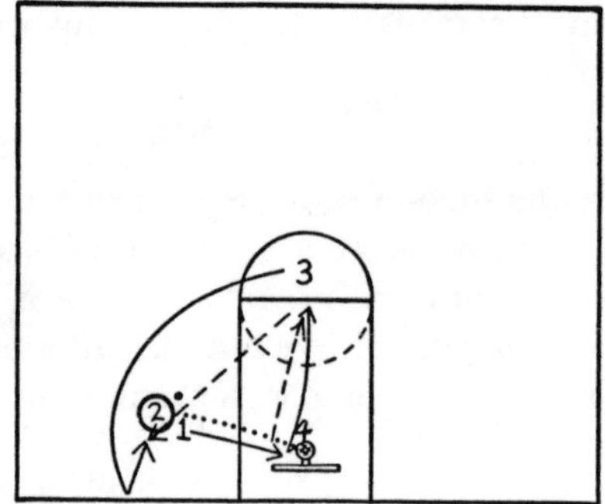

COACH CLEM HASKINS—WESTERN KENTUCKY UNIVERSITY

Coach Haskins has been coaching at Western Kentucky for three years. He has a won/lost record of 52 wins and 34 losses. His teams won the Ohio Valley championship in 1980–81 and 1981–1982. He was selected NBC Rookie Coach of the Year in 1981 and O.V.C. Coach of the Year in 1981.

FOUR-MAN SHOOTING DRILL

Purpose: To improve shooting on the move
Personnel and Equipment Needed: Four players, two basketballs and one basket
Teaching Points: 1) Move toward the ball at game speed. 2) Catch the ball with knees bent. 3) Plant inside foot and pivot to square up to the basket. 4) Explode for the jumper.
Directions: Players number 1 and 3 have basketballs and are designated as passers. They should concentrate on making a good two-handed chest pass. Number 2 is designated as the shooter and should work hard for the 45 seconds allotted for each shooter. Number 2 will make a hard "v-cut" to the elbow on number 1's side, catching the ball with his knees bent and pivoting on his inside foot to explode for the jumper. Then he will "v-cut" to the elbow on number 3's side. Number 4 is the rebounder and passes the ball back to number 1 while number 2 is catching the pass from number 3. Rotate the players so that each has the opportunity to shoot. Have manager record how many shots are made by each shooter.

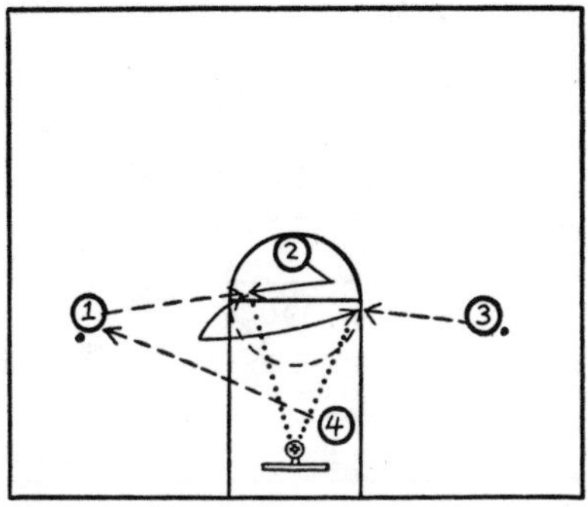

COACH MARK REINER—BROOKLYN COLLEGE

Coach Reiner has been coaching for fourteen years. Two of those fourteen years have been at the college level. He has compiled a won/lost record of 192 wins and 71 losses. His teams have won several championships, including Division III NCAA Regional championship in 1982. That same year his team finished third at the Division III national tournament. He was nominated for NCAA Division III Coach of the Year in 1982.

"DAILY NINETY" JUMP SHOT DRILL

Purpose: To improve jump shooting ability
Personnel and Equipment Needed: One player, one ball at each basket
Teaching Points: 1) Turning and facing the basket properly. 2) Have ball in correct position. 3) No dribbling in drill. 4) Following missed shots for lay-ups.
Directions: Players start at any of the six spots in the diagram, with the ball facing away from the basket. They turn so that they are properly facing the basket with the ball in the correct position above the head. They take the shot and head to the basket as soon as the ball leaves their hand. If they miss, they retrieve the ball and shoot again without dribbling. Hopefully, this will be a lay-up. If they make the shot, they carry the ball back to the same spot and continue until they shoot 15 shots from all six spots.

This can be used as a pre-practice shooting drill. You may change the position or number of spots to fit your situation.

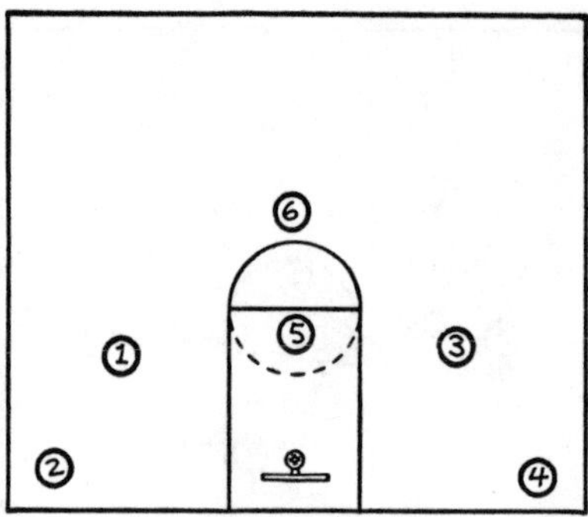

COACH MIKE SHAKER—MESSIAH COLLEGE

Coach Shaker has been coaching for twenty years. Fourteen of those twenty years have been at Messiah College where he has compiled a won/lost record of 238 wins and 149 losses. His teams were National Christian College Athletic Association District champions in 1973, 1975, and 1979. They finished third at the NCCAA national tournament in 1975. He won the Schoefield Award in 1971, was NCCAA National Coach of the Year in 1974, and NAIA District Coach of the Year in 1979.

"K" OFF THE DRIBBLE DRILL

Purpose: To improve and isolate shooting off the dribble
Personnel and Equipment Needed: Two to twelve players, one or two basketballs, two pylons at free throw lines extended four feet and a basket.
Teaching Points: 1) Make final dribble be in front of you on shooting hip. 2) Get inside heel down to get balance for proper shot technique. 3) Proper eye transfer to the basket for target. 4) Rebounder learns to rebound the angles.
Directions: Individual—Have the players get in groups of two and go to each basket. Have two pylons at each basket foul line, extended four feet. One player is the shooter and the other is the rebounder. The shooter starts with the ball and makes two dribbles to the baseline for the jumper. The rebounder gets the ball and passes it back to the shooter who is back at the pylon pitter-pattering. Now the shooter takes one dribble to the elbow or lane line for a jumper. The rebounder returns the

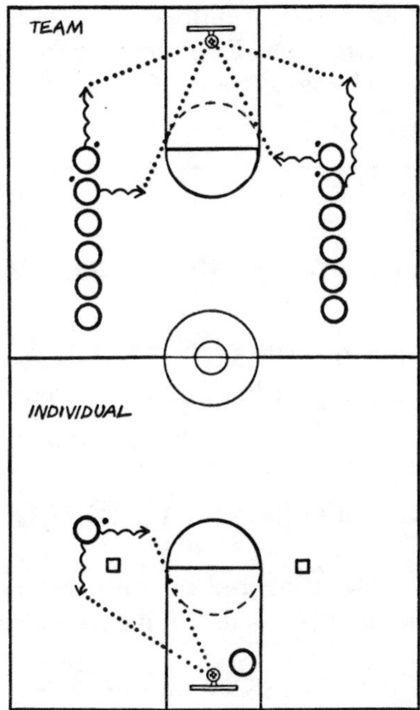

ball back to the shooter at the pylon. This continues for 30 seconds, alternating shots at the baseline and at the elbow. After the 30 seconds, the two players switch positions. After each player has shot from one side, they switch sides and continue the drill. The drill takes two minutes. Learn to "K" that shot with confidence in these two critical areas. Make sure to record the results.

Team—Start with six players in a line on each side of the free throw line extended four feet. The first two players in each line have basketballs. The first player in one line dribbles to the baseline for the shot, while the first player in the other line goes to the elbow for the shot. The next player in each line goes to the other shooting area, waiting only until the player before them shoots. *Key:* Shooter follows shot but only to facilitate continuity of the drill. You must emphasize good shooting balance and not following a miss, or you will miss. Take your rebound to the opposite line with two or three hard dribbles. Work on crossover dribble and then pass to the next man in line without a ball as drill continues.

Variations: Have one line go only to the baseline while the other line goes to the elbow. Then, after a certain number of scores, switch shots.

Key item: Chart team and/or individual shooting on this drill as an indicator of shooting percentage. Don't let players think they are shooting better than they really are. Use the facts to the best advantage.

COACH DON C. PURDY—BELMONT COLLEGE

Coach Purdy has been coaching for sixteen years. Ten of those sixteen years have been at the college level as either an assistant or head coach. He has a won/lost record at Belmont College of 77 wins and 73 losses.

SHOOTING STAR DRILL

Purpose: To improve cutting and shooting technique
Personnel and Equipment Needed: Five to fifteen players, two basketballs and half-court
Teaching Points: 1) Make proper cuts off of the high post. 2) Make correct chest and overhead passes and handoffs. 3) Keep body under control for jump shots.

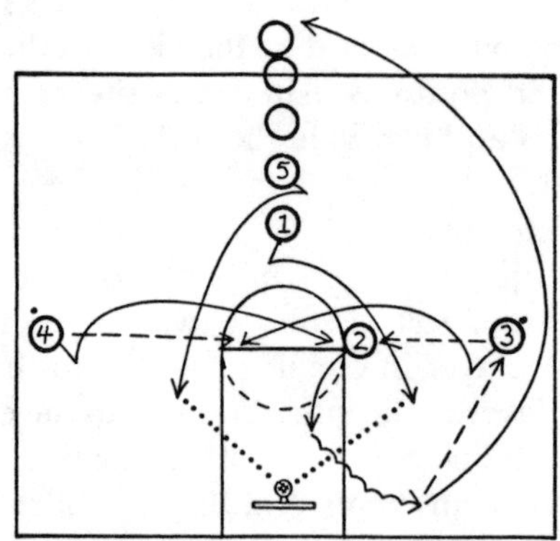

Directions: Begin the drill with one player in each of the following spots: 2, 3, and 4. The remainder of the team lines up behind the player at the number 1 spot. The player in the number 2 spot assumes the post position. The players at numbers 3 and 4 have balls. Number 3 starts the drill with a chest pass to number 2 and cuts to the opposite post. Number 1 fakes right and cuts off numbers 3 and 2. Number 2 gives the ball (handoff) to number 1 for a jump shot. Number 2 rebounds the shot and passes the ball back to number 1 who, after the shot, has assumed the position vacated by number 3. He then goes to the end of the line at the top of the key. Number 4 makes a chest pass to number 3 at the post as soon as number 3 establishes position. Number 4 cuts to the opposite post and number 5 fakes left and cuts right off numbers 4 and 3. Number 3 gives the ball (handoff) to number 5 for a jump shot. Number 3 rebounds the shot and passes the ball back to number 5 who moves to the spot vacated by number 4. He then goes to the end of the line at the top of the key. The drill continues in this manner for as long as you like.

Variations:

(1) Instead of shooting the jumper, the cutter passes the ball to the high post rolling to the basket.
(2) The post fakes a handoff to the cutter, squares up, and shoots a jumper.
(3) The post fakes a handoff to the cutter and then hits the cutter in the corner for a jump shot.
(4) The cutter, after receiving the pass from the post, fakes the shot and passes the ball back to the high post for a jumper.

COACH JESSE R. LILLY—GLENVILLE STATE COLLEGE

Coach Lilly has been coaching for twenty years. Seventeen of those years have been at Glenville State College. He has compiled a won/lost record of 308 wins and 251 losses. His teams won the West Virginia Intercollegiate Athletic Conference championships in 1970 and 1972. He was selected as West Virginia Colleges Coach of the Year and WVIAC Coach of the Year.

FIVE-MAN PIVOT SHOOTING DRILL

Purpose: To teach pivoting—square up to the basket
Personnel and Equipment Needed: Three to five players, one coach, two basketballs and a basket.
Teaching Points: 1) Make a correct pivot—fake—drive to the right or left. 2) Shoot a power lay-up or pull up for a jump shot. 3) Rebound any missed shot.

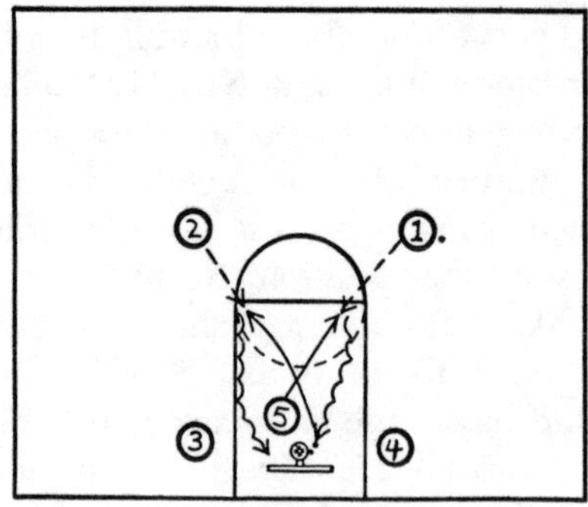

Directions: Number 5 is the shooter. On the whistle, he races to the ball—a pass from number 1. He catches the ball—squares up to the basket. Then he fakes right and goes left, using his left hand to shoot a lay-up. He rebounds a miss if one occurs. Number 4 rebounds the make and passes the ball back out to number 1. Meanwhile, number 5 races toward number 2, receives the pass, squares up, fakes left, goes right and shoots a lay-up. He then returns to number 1 and repeats the movement. This goes on at a fast pace for two minutes. Then players rotate positions.

Variations:

(1) Numbers 1 and 2 can lay the ball on the floor and roll it slowly, right or left for number 5 to retrieve. He squares up, fakes and drives to the basket.
(2) Move this same drill to the baseline.
(3) You may spread this drill out and make it a half-court, loose-ball drill. Have numbers 3 or 4 roll the ball in the direction of the center line and have number 5 retrieve it, square up and make a pass back to either 3 or 4, and then get a return pass for a jumper.

COACH TOM PENDERS—FORDHAM UNIVERSITY

Coach Penders has been coaching for sixteen years. Thirteen of those sixteen years have been at the college level. He has a won/lost record at the college level of 171 wins and 148 losses. His teams won the

ECAC College Division championship and the ECAC Metro championship in 1981. He was selected NABC District 2, Division I, Coach of the Year in 1981 and New York Metro Coach of the Year in 1981.

POST MOVES AND PERIMETER SHOOTING DRILL

Purpose: To improve post moves for the big men and perimeter cutting, passing and shooting for the guards
Personnel and Equipment Needed: One coach, one manager, entire team of players, four basketballs and two baskets
Teaching Points: Big men: Make hard flash cut to low or side post. Guards: 1) Make sharp "v" cut to get open to receive a pass; 2) Square to the basket to shoot the ball.

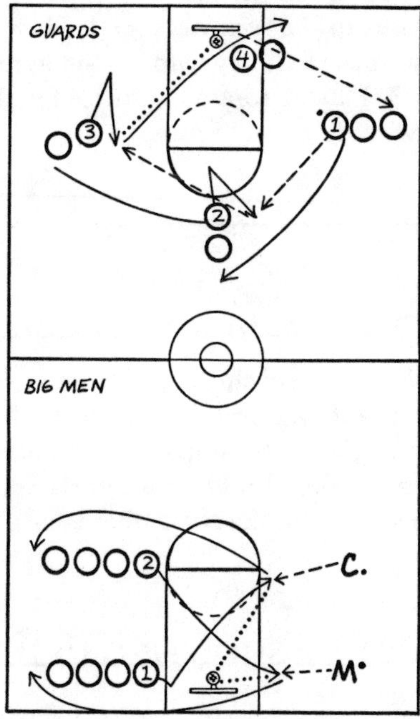

Directions: Big men—Have the players line up in two lines, one at the low post and one at the high post on the opposite side of the key from the feeders (coach and manager). The low post line (line number 1) cuts across the key to the high post, receives the pass, spins, shows the ball, pumps and shoots. The shooter follows his shot and outlets the ball back to the feeder. The high post line (line number 2) cuts off the tail of line number 1 and flashes to the low post. After receiving the pass, the shooter either shoots a jump hook or turns and makes a power move. He then rebounds his shot and outlets the ball back to the feeder. The two players then go to the end of the opposite line. The drill continues for three minutes and then the shooters are moved to the opposite side.

Variation: Have shooting lines flash straight across (low post to low post and high post to high post).

Guards: At the second basket, have your guards divide up into four lines (one point, two wings and one rebounder). Number 1 starts the drill by passing the ball to number 2 who has made a good "v" cut to get open. Number 2 then passes the ball to number 3 who has made a hard "v" cut to get open. Number 3, as he receives the ball, plants his inside foot, squares to the basket and shoots the jumper. Number 4 rebounds the shot and passes out to the next number 1. Have two basketballs in line number 1 and start the second group as soon as number 2 has passed the ball to number 3. Players rotate clockwise for three minutes, then rotate counterclockwise for another three.

COACH RUSS REILLY—MIDDLEBURY COLLEGE

Coach Reilly has been coaching for fifteen years all at the college level, as either an assistant or a head coach. He has been a staff member at several summer basketball camps and clinics throughout New England. He had an article, "Building a Fundamentally Sound Man-to-Man Defense," published in the November issue of the *Athletic Journal* in 1976.

POST UP SHOOTING DRILL

Purpose: To improve low post moves and shooting
Personnel and Equipment Needed: A minimum of three players, one basketball and one basket
Teaching Points: 1) Execute a sharp "v" cut. 2) Catch the ball with both feet parallel so that either foot can be a pivot foot.

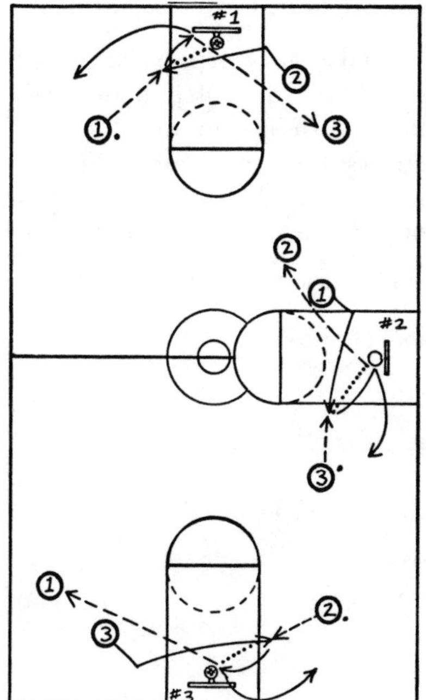

Directions: Three players start in the three areas shown. Number 1 has the basketball and to start the drill, number 2 makes a "v" cut to the opposite low post area. Number 1 passes him the ball and he executes one of the moves on page 208. After he shoots, he rebounds the ball, passes it out to number 3 and moves out to replace number 1. On number 2's pass to number 3, number 1 starts his "v" cut to the opposite low post area (see Diagram #2). Number 3 passes him the ball and he executes the same move as number 2. He then rebounds his shot, passes it to number 2 and moves out to replace number 3. On number 1's pass to number 2, number 3 begins his "v" cut to the opposite low post area (see Diagram #3). Number 2 passes the ball to number 3 who performs the same move as the two before him. He then rebounds his shot and passes the ball to number 1. On the pass to number 1, number 2 starts his "v" cut to the opposite low post area. This time number 2 will execute another offensive move from the list below. The drill continues until all the moves have been performed by all three players. It should take about five minutes to complete this drill.

The moves that are to be executed:

1. Inside ball fake, drop step, power lay-up.
2. Outside ball fake, drop step, hook shot.
3. Quick inside turn and a jump shot.
4. Quick outside turn and a jump shot.
5. Quick inside turn, shot fake, crossover step and power shot.
6. Quick outside turn, shot fake, crossover step and hook shot.

Variation: Add defense to make the drill three-on-three.

Part VIII

TEAM DEVELOPMENT DRILLS

COACH GORDON FOSTER—LEBANON VALLEY COLLEGE

Coach Foster has been coaching for twenty-nine years. Two of those twenty-nine years have been at the college level. He has an overall won/lost record of 543 wins and 134 losses. His teams have won seventeen league championships. He was named Coach of the Year in 1956, 1957, 1958, 1962, 1963, 1964, 1966, 1967, 1969, 1970, 1971, 1972, 1975, 1978, 1981 and 1982.

"VALLEY" DRILL

Purpose: To teach the skills necessary for screening inside, rebounding and outletting the ball

Personnel and Equipment Needed: A minimum of ten players, one basketball and the entire floor

Teaching Points: 1) Offense must wait on the screen. 2) Get your shot off the pass. 3) Be selective on the shot. 4) Defense calls out the shot. 5) Block-out properly. 6) Make a good outlet pass. 7) Fill the lanes on the break.

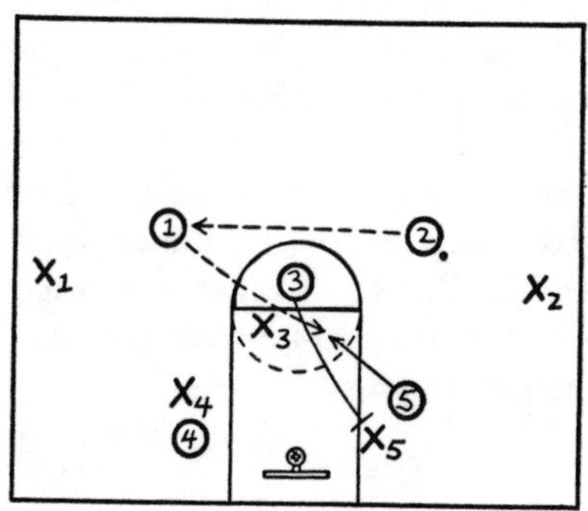

Directions: Divide the ten players into two teams. One team is on offense, the other is on defense. The two offensive guards (O1 and O2) position themselves in the guard spots out front. The two defensive guards (X1 and X2) position themselves in the outlet positions on the wings.

The remaining three players on both teams play three-on-three inside the key area. The three offensive men will play without the ball and will down-screen until they get open. The guards will pass the ball to the open man. If the defensive man is too close to the shooter, he throws the ball back out to one of the guards and they continue to screen inside to get a man open for a good shot.

After a shot, the three defensive men block out the three offensive men and go for the rebound. Upon securing the rebound, they outlet the ball to either X1 or X2, depending on which side the ball was rebounded. After the outlet, X3, X4 and X5 fill the lanes on the break to the other end. O1 and O2 form a tandem defense until O3, O4 and O5 can get back to help. If they cannot score off the break, they go into their transition offense and try to score. If they do not score on the first shot, play is stopped and the team with the ball executes the same drill at that end. If they score on the break or transition offense, the team that scored sets up the drill at that end. This drill should last about eight minutes.

COACH RALPH H. MILLER—OREGON STATE UNIVERSITY

Coach Miller has been coaching for thirty-six years. Thirty-three of those thirty-six have been at the college level. He has a won/lost record of 242 wins and 125 losses at Oregon State and 620 wins and 326 losses overall. His teams have won a Kansas High School state championship, one Missouri Valley Conference championship, two Big Ten Conference championships and three Pacific Ten Conference championships. He has received Coach of the Year honors from the Missouri Valley Conference twice, the Big Ten Conference twice, the Pacific Eight once, and the Pacific Ten three times. He has also received national Coach of the Year honors twice.

THREE-ON-THREE FULL-COURT DRILL

Purpose: To teach players how to play the game on a full-court and a half-court basis

Personnel and Equipment Needed: A minimum of six players, one basketball and the entire floor

Teaching Points: 1) Stress good passes and cuts to the ball. 2) Defense should be aggressive, but play position. 3) Emphasize good shot selection. 4) Make sure you block off the boards.

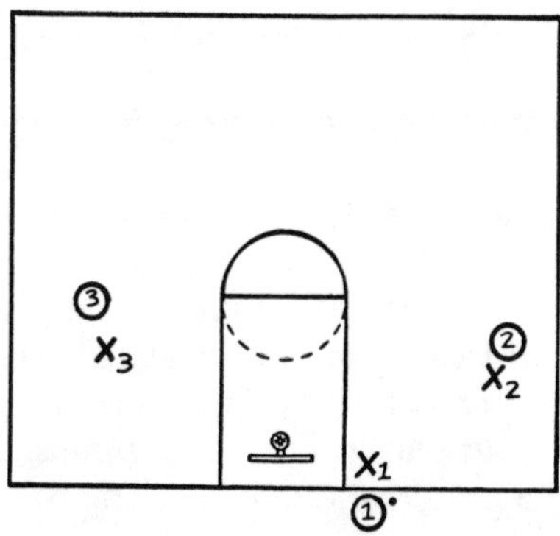

Directions: Divide your six players into two teams of three each. O1 has the ball underneath the basket. The drill begins with O1 trying to inbounds the ball to either O2 or O3. They are to advance the ball down the floor and try to score at the other end. X1, X2 and X3 play defense on O1, O2 and O3 and make it difficult for the offense to accomplish their purposes. The offense has only one attempt to score. Play stops after each attempt, the offense becomes defense and the defense becomes offense. You can exchange all six players after one trip up and down the floor. All offensive and defensive skill executions are involved in the drill except for free throw shooting. All rules and theory for individual and team play on offense and defense can be learned and stressed in this one drill. *Note:* The center court line may or may not be used so that the ball cannot be inbounded directly across that line.

COACH GARY COLSON—UNIVERSITY OF NEW MEXICO

Coach Colson has been coaching at the collegiate level for twenty-four years. He has an overall won/lost record of 380 wins and 250 losses. His teams won the NAIA District 25 championship twice and the West

Coast Athletic Conference title once. He was named Atlanta Tip-Off Club Coach of the Year in 1968 and West Coast Athletic Conference Coach of the Year in 1976.

PRESSURE WORKUPS DRILL

Purpose: To learn to perform under pressure both offensively and defensively

Personnel and Equipment Needed: Two or more coaches, a minimum of fifteen players, one basketball and the entire floor

Teaching Points: 1) Offense must not turn the ball over. 2) Offense must not force a shot. 3) Defense must deny at all times. 4) Defense must block out. 5) Defense must talk. 6) Defense must not get blown by.

Directions: Divide your players into three groups: an offensive team, a defensive team and a group on the bench. The two teams out on the

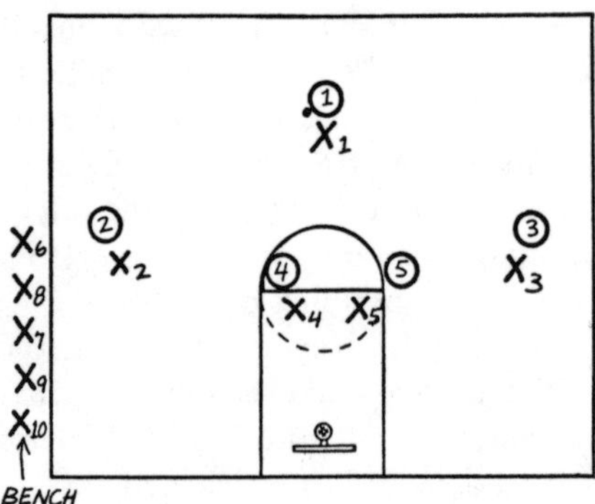

floor work against each other half-court. The defense plays an aggressive man-to-man and the offense runs their half-court man offense. The idea of the drill is to get the offense to execute their offense without making a turnover or forcing a bad shot while under extreme defensive pressure. The rules are as follows: 1) The offense remains out as long as they do not cause a turnover or force a bad shot; if they do, they go to the end of their line on the bench. 2) The only exception is on an entry pass to the wing. Here, if a turnover occurs, both the point and wing go to the bench. 3) The defense is replaced for the following: failure to deny on the wings, failure to block-out, failure to talk on defense, and if the offense blows by them.

The rotation of players is as follows: The bench goes to defense, the defense goes to offense if they forced a turnover or bad shot, or to the bench if they failed in one of their four assignments previously discussed. The offense goes to the bench for a turnover or forced shot. The coaches will need to police this at the beginning, but soon the players on the bench will be doing it. The players on the bench should be in three different groups as they wait; point guards, wings and posts. It is recommended that you use this for 20 to 30 minutes a day.

Variation:

1) It can be used full court by stopping play after a score or defensive rebound and giving the ball to the offense to take back the other way.
2) You can adjust the reasons for being bumped off defense and offense to the bench to fit your philosophy or areas that your team needs work on.